PITCHFORK

FREDERICA STEINBERG

ONION
RIVER

PRESS

Burlington, Vermont

Onion River Press
89 Church Street
Burlington, VT 05401
info@onionriverpress.com
www.onionriverpress.com

ISBN: 978-1-966607-05-2 Paperback
Library of Congress Control Number: 2025905610

For my grandchildren: Jake, Maya, Julia, and Jack

CONTENTS

THE BET

Stubby Murphy was stubby, that's for sure. His two short legs held up his square body, one leg on each side. He was a jolly fellow with a broad smile and twinkly eyes. Sometimes he reminded me of Santa, but without the beard. His real first name was William, but everyone called him Stubby. He didn't mind.

He was a large animal vet, and he took care of my father's horses. He and his family also rode, usually Morgans, and competed in the 100 Mile Ride that took place every Labor Day in Woodstock, Vermont.

When I was eight years old, Stubby and my father made a bet. Would my mother place in the 100 Mile? My father was sure she would, but Stubby wasn't so sure. Because Martial Maid, my mother's mount, was off the track, Stubby thought the mare might blow up, get too excited, wear herself out. This was the first time my mother had competed in this ride, and Stubby thought that maybe inexperience would play its part, as well.

Not only did my mother agree to join my father and me in this ride, but she would also have to condition my father's mare, Miss Chance, because he was at work all day. My father could be persuasive, but this persuasive?

I was at Camp Teela-Wooket in Roxbury, Vermont, a horse camp for girls, so I couldn't help. Nosey, the horse I would ride, was at camp with me.

So, the bet was on. Stubby would pay my father one hundred dollars if my mother placed in the top ten. If not, Stubby would collect from my father.

The summer went by quickly. In late August, Nosey and I returned home from camp, and soon the first day of the 100 Mile arrived.

Day one went smoothly. All three horses finished in time. My mother had done a good job.

Day two went moderately well. Miss Chance was tired, and my father encouraged my mother and me to ride on and not to wait for him. Seven hours later, my mother and I crossed the finish line, my father one hour late. Stubby began to worry. Would he lose one hundred dollars?

That evening, my father announced that he might scratch.

"Miss Chance is exhausted, and I hate to push her. But I'll wait till the morning and take a second look."

Day three arrived. It was six o'clock in the morning, and my father did take a second look at his horse and talked to the vet. Every year, the ride hired two vets to oversee the health of the horses.

"Roger, take it very easy. You can always stop," the vets said.

"Okay, that's what I'll do."

At seven, we tacked up the horses and left at the appointed time. A time-keeper gave us the signal, and off we went. Miss Chance soon tired, and my father quit.

"Keep going," he said. "Your two horses are fit and healthy. I'll walk Miss Chance to the Shallow's—just down the road—and call for a trailer."

So my mother and I continued. The forecast was rain, but we thought we'd be back before the deluge. After all, day three was only twenty miles. But ten miles along, the heavens opened, and it poured, and I mean poured. We did have raincoats, but the rain penetrated them, and we were soon soaked through. In those days, nobody wore a helmet, so our hair was sopping wet and cold.

Mile fifteen—five to go. Horses covered forty miles on day one and forty miles on day two, each in seven hours, but on day three, they went twenty miles in three hours—a faster pace. So we were zipping right along.

Martial Maid couldn't wait to return to the barn, and my mother was having trouble controlling her. They crossed the finish line galloping—my mother's hair was flying, she was soaked through, and she was hanging on for dear life. Everyone applauded. She had covered those last five miles in record time.

"Helen, you did it!" My father grabbed Martial Maid's reins and helped my poor, exhausted, drenched mother dismount.

"Jesus," she said. "Thank God that's over."

That afternoon, all the horses and riders lined up in the ring waiting to see who won and who placed in all three divisions: heavyweight, lightweight, and junior. My mother rode in the lightweight, and I obviously in the junior. We dutifully joined the other horses and waited. It has stopped raining, which was a blessing.

"In the heavyweight division, in tenth place..."

"And in ninth place..." And so it went. Now the lightweight division.

"In the lightweight division, in tenth place..."

"And in ninth place..."

"And in eighth place..."

Stubby and my father were standing outside the ring, leaning against the rails. Stubby shifted his weight and smiled.

"Roger, you know Helen won't place higher than eighth." My father looked at him.

"You think? We'll see."

"And in seventh place..."

"And in sixth place..."

Stubby laughed and held out his hand.

"Hundred dollars? I'm waiting!"

"And in fifth place..."

My father pulled out the hundred-dollar bill and shrugged.

"Well, Stubby, a good bet, but looks like you've won."

"And in fourth place, Helen Maher riding Martial Maid."

Stubby gasped. "What? What? My God, she did it."

"Yup, she did." My father laughed loudly. "I knew that mare was doing well, but I didn't know this well." And my father held out his hand, giving Stubby a friendly whack on his back with his other.

"Stubby," my father said, "have faith!"

My mother beamed as the ringmaster pinned a beautiful white ribbon on Martial Maid's bridle. She waved at my father and Stubby and patted Martial Maid on her neck.

I placed fifth in the junior division that year. I was thrilled because this was the first time I had competed. The following year, Nosey and I won. She was a tough, strong mare and would have done well in more 100 Mile rides, but she hurt her knee jumping a stone wall and had to be retired. I rode other horses in many other rides, but none did as well as Nosey.

My mother and I left the ring and dismounted.

"Helen, incredible job," my father said as he hugged her. "Fantastic."

"Thanks. The mare just kept on going. All I had to do was to hang on."

My father turned to Stubby. "What do you think now?"

"Well, looks like you won the bet."

My mother looked at both of them. "Who won?"

Pitchfork

My father and Stubby laughed as Stubby handed my mother a crisp one-hundred dollar bill.

"A tough way to win a hundred," said my mother, "but I'll take it." And that was the last time she rode in the 100 Mile.

$400.00

We headed down the hill toward the ring with one fence to go. Martial Maid, a 10-year-old thoroughbred, and I had sailed over all the post and rail fences and had one chicken coop to go. She loved to jump and easily cleared the fences. I whispered in her ear, "Great job, great job" and patted her on the shoulder as we galloped along.

Suddenly, without warning, down she went. I somersaulted off the saddle and landed safely to the left, quickly regaining my feet. Martial Maid scrambled to her feet as well. What had happened? Had she stumbled? I waited a minute or two, then slowly led her down the hill.

My father met us at the bottom. "Are you okay?"

"Yes," I said. "But I have no idea what happened."

My father moved his hands down each leg then asked me to jog her, which I did.

"Hm, nothing I can detect."

I led her to the barn, untacked her, and rubbed her down. I filled her water bucket and gave her a slice of hay. She munched happily.

My father called Dr. Robinson, our vet, who arrived about an hour later.

"She must have fainted," he said. "I can't see anything wrong. I'll check her again tomorrow. She may have had a heart attack."

"Heart attack?" My father frowned. "Then it could be serious."

"Yes," said Dr. Robinson. "It could be. Keep her stabled here for the night, and I'll check her first thing in the morning."

I rode Miss Chance in the afternoon on the same outside course. No mishaps this time, and we won our class. We also entered the equitation class and handy hunter class. Miss Chance wasn't a "handy" hunter, so the blue ribbon went to someone else. But I did earn a blue ribbon in equitation.

Around four o'clock, I started for home on Miss Chance, a four-mile ride. My father checked on Martial Maid, who seemed happy and content, then drove home.

He and I returned to the Windsor Horse Show stables at seven o'clock the next morning to discover an empty stall, the door bolted shut—like my father had left it. What on Earth had happened? Someone stole our horse? She was on her way to New Jersey? New York? Where could Martial Maid be?

We drove around, asked people, but got no information about her whereabouts. My father called the town police officer, who said he'd have a look. Hours later, still no Martial Maid.

My father and I had a quick bite to eat at the Windsor Diner, then continued our search. By two o'clock, we were really worried. We returned to the Windsor Horse Show stables and retraced our steps. Still no luck.

We drove back to our house, parked the car, and walked into the house.

"Helen," said my father to my mother, "we still can't locate Martial Maid."

"Look out the window," she said, smiling.

Martial Maid was munching grass in the paddock. We hoped she was looking sheepish, but I don't think she was. She had jumped out of the stall and leisurely made her way home.

"When did you notice her?"

"Only minutes ago," said my mother.

Dr. Robinson had no idea what had caused the mare to fall, so that was the end of it. Martial Maid continued her illustrious horse show career until we noticed a slight limp that became severe osteoarthritis. She was eighteen.

"Frederica, it's time," my father said. I'd heard this many times before, and Martial Maid would soon join her friends in the lower horse pasture graveyard. "Yes," I answered, "I know."

I wandered into the tack room and gently removed her bridle from the hook on the wall and added it to the others in the tack trunk, now quite full. I gazed at the ribbons she'd won, all neatly nailed to the wall. "Martial Maid," I said out loud, "not bad for an OTTB (off-the-track thoroughbred) my father had purchased for $400.00."

The Yellow Pad

"You'll see the instructions on the workbench," my father said as he walked toward his car.

"Okay," I said.

I was home from boarding school, having just completed my freshman year. During the summer months, I trained for the Labor Day 100 Mile trail ride, competed in weekend horse shows, rode in three-day events, and schooled a couple of young horses. I also gave riding lessons to a few young girls in the neighborhood. I charged three dollars an hour.

My father's car disappeared down the driveway. I walked into the garage, and the lined yellow pad—attached to a clipboard—sat solemnly on the workbench, staring at me like it did every morning. Every entry, neatly written in a straight column, started with a capital letter and ended with a period.

Frederica—
1. Put Martial Maid and Fireglow in the lower pasture; leave Kaya in.
2. Muck out the stalls—fresh bedding in each.
3. Ride Miss Chance one hour—trot ten minutes, walk five.
4. Ride Nosey two hours—trot fifteen minutes, walk five.
5. Clean out their hoofs.
6. Clean the bridles; pay attention to the bits.
7. Prepare for your three students.
8. Sweep the driveway.
9. Lead Martial Maid and Fireglow back to the barn at five o'clock.
10. Feed the horses at five thirty; make sure each gets plenty of hay and water.

I looked up at the screwdrivers, hammers, and wrenches, all neatly hanging from nails above the workbench. A whisk broom complemented this assortment of tools because my father swept the workbench morning and night. I ripped the page from the yellow pad, folded it, and stuffed it into my back pocket. I left the garage and walked across the driveway past the house and toward the paddock.

It was a beautiful, warm July day; I noticed a robin peck for worms then hop into my mother's flower bed that bordered the paddock fence. My mother loved to weed, and her efforts paid off. Not a weed in sight!

I opened the gate and walked through the paddock to the barn. The horses whinnied as I approached. After leading the two horses to the lower pasture, I began mucking out, which I enjoyed. I filled the wheelbarrow again and again with manure and wet, dirty shavings that I dumped onto the manure pile to the right of the barn door. I left a few damp shavings in each stall. My father would never know. Defiance! Disobedience! These words danced merrily in my head as I covered the damp shavings with dry shavings. A small victory, but a victory nonetheless.

I led Miss Chance out of her stall, cross-tied her, and brushed her off. She gave me a gentle nudge as I saddled her up. A kind mare, she was easy to handle and to ride. Up the hill we went to the long, beautiful field that had recently been hayed. I looked at my watch. Here we go. Ten minutes trot, five minutes walk, ten minutes trot, five minutes walk. One hour later, we returned to the barn. I unsaddled Miss Chance, brushed her off, cleaned out her hoofs, and led her into a small paddock next to the barn.

Nosey wasn't as good-natured. But we got along fine for the next two hours, following my father's yellow pad instructions. I cleaned the bridles and bits, then hung them up in the tack room. I removed the instructions from my back pocket and checked off the first six items. It was one thirty, time for lunch.

My mother was at her weekly bridge group, so I had the place to myself. I made a peanut butter sandwich and sat down at the kitchen table. Horse photographs hung from the walls: my father jumping his dark brown thoroughbred, my mother astride her Morgan, horses munching grass in the pasture. Photographs of me on various horses predominated. I stared at the one taken six years ago, when I was eight years old, riding Honey, a black-and-white Shetland pony about twelve hands high. I still owned the jodhpur boots that I wore in this photo. I looked at that little girl and wondered what she was thinking. I took a deep breath and pulled my eyes away. The sandwich wasn't as good as I had hoped, but it satisfied my hunger.

A car pulled into the driveway. It was two o'clock, time for my first lesson.

"Hello, Susie," I said. "I'm all ready for you." Susie, my youngest student, was a beginner. She was timid so we took it very slowly.

"Brush Kaya's shoulder like this," I told her. Kaya was the old lady in the barn and as reliable as any horse could be. "Good," I said, as Susie slowly pushed the brush up and down Kaya's shoulder. "Probably it's best to go in one direction," I added. And she did. Kaya, however, was perfectly happy if the brush went up or down or sideways. That's the kind of horse she was.

Nine dollars and two students later, I attacked the driveway, the end-of-the-day job. Sweep, sweep, sweep. I crossed off another item.

Five o'clock arrived. Martial Maid and Fireglow obediently waited for me at the gate. I fed the horses, making sure each got enough hay and plenty of water. Each bucket had to be filled. But I managed and finished all the chores by five forty-five. Smiling and smugly satisfied, I slowly walked back to the garage. I could claim victory, once again, and check everything off. The yellow pad was waiting for me, as was my father. I dug into my pocket, removed the creased yellow piece of paper, and placed it on the pad.

"Frederica," my father said as he flattened the piece of yellow paper and read down the list, pointing to each item with the middle finger of his right hand. "Everything done?"

"Yes." I nodded.

"Good."

I stood still and waited. My father shifted his weight, briefcase in one hand and a pencil in his other.

"Frederica, you finished everything?" He looked at me, tilting his head and smiling.

"Yes, I did." I met his gaze.

My father put his briefcase on the floor and began a new list. I watched him as he carefully began each entry with a capital letter and ended each with a period. I wondered how a yellow paper pad could rule my life, but it did.

The Outline

I stood outside my dorm at Concord Academy, waiting for my father. I looked down at my polished black riding boots with glossy patent leather tops, a birthday gift from him three years ago. They fit snugly, so I needed boot hooks to pull them on. My black velvet hunt cap, beige breeches, stock, and silver stock pin, also a gift from my father, completed my outfit. It was ten o'clock a.m.

"Freddy, where's your dad?" Wendy, one of my two roommates, appeared around the corner, carrying her book bag.

"Not here yet," I answered. "Where are you going?"

"Library. You know, that darn English paper due tomorrow." She grimaced and walked away. I did indeed know. I had an outline, but that was all. I looked at my watch, moving it up and down my wrist. The maroon leather strap needed another hole, just a little too big for my wrist.

Where was he? On Sunday the bars were closed, so I shouldn't have to worry about that. But worry I did. I gazed down the street, searching for the big grey hay truck that doubled for a horse box. Wooden partitions created three spaces for horses, the fourth horse standing crossways at the back. This was Nosey's place, and for all her crankiness, she didn't seem to mind.

Today, the third of November, was chilly. I slipped on my brown leather gloves, relieved that I had found them in my bottom drawer hiding under wool cardigans. Sometimes I hunted without gloves, but today I needed them. The sky was slightly overcast, and I wondered if it might rain. Hunting in raw, rainy weather wasn't my idea of fun.

Ten minutes later, the hay truck turned the far corner onto Main Street and stopped in front of my dorm. My father turned off the engine, got out, and walked toward me. Was he okay? I thought so.

"Hello, Frederica, here I am." He gave me a kiss on the cheek. "Exams?"

"Okay," I said, "except for Latin." I hated Latin, and I hated my teacher, Miss Perkins, who had her favorites—I was not one of them. My father loved Latin and couldn't understand why none of his three children didn't share his appreciation for this (in my opinion) outdated and dead language.

"I'm sure you did fine," my father said. I didn't contradict him.

"Frederica, I have to use the john. I'll be right out." I hoped the house mistress, Mrs. Shepard, wouldn't see him, especially in his riding attire. A stern and commanding woman, she followed all the rules. All visitors, including family members, had to sign in. We girls tiptoed around her, making sure our beds were made properly, our clothes hung up, and our hair combed. "Lights out" meant "lights out." No wiggle room!

I walked to the back of the truck, stood on the back fender, and looked in. Both horses were tacked up and happily munching hay. I returned to the front and peered in. My father's well-worn riding boots stood on the floor, their heavy wooden trees poking out of the tops. His pink riding jacket lay on the passenger's seat, along with his velvet hunt cap.

"Frederica," my father said as he emerged from the front door. "Do you have everything? We need to go."

"I'm all set." He didn't mention Mrs. Shepard, so I was saved from that indignity.

He climbed into the driver's seat and turned on the ignition, and off we went. I sat quietly beside him, having moved his jacket and cap to the side.

"It'll be a good day," my father said. "I'm sure of it."

"Yes," I said, looking out the window at the darkening sky.

As we drove out of Concord and headed for Groton, I thought about the English paper that was due tomorrow. I had written a fairly detailed outline, but I needed at least two more hours to write a decent paper. Would I get those two hours?

We arrived at the Groton Inn in good time. Riders were tacking up and mounting. I noticed a man struggling with a black horse that wouldn't stand still. Another rider came to his rescue, held the man's horse, and he was finally able to mount. I'd have to avoid that guy.

My father and I let the tailgate down and unloaded the horses. He adjusted the throat latch on Prompted's bridle then tightened the girth. "Frederica, hold him while I mount." I then checked my girth and quickly mounted. My father chatted with other riders, some of whom I had met over the years. Soon the inn waiter arrived with glasses of port, the traditional "stirrup cup" for all the riders. My father gulped his down and asked for another.

After three hours of hunting, we returned to the inn for the hunt breakfast, always accompanied with liquor. After loading the horses, we wandered into the inn, and my father headed for the bar. "Great day," he said to the bartender, who smiled.

"Dad, we really have to go," I said, approaching the bar. "I need time to finish my paper."

"Frederica, we'll leave in a few minutes." He wandered across the room, chatting and laughing.

I found a chair and sat down and said goodbye to my English paper. What would Mr. Eddy say? Would I get an extension because I was fox-hunting with my father? I doubted it.

And I was right.

BACK AT SCHOOL

The train pulled into the station at four o'clock, and my mother waved at me from the platform. I was fifteen and home for Thanksgiving vacation.

"'Freddy, so glad you're home." We hugged, and I followed her to the car, suitcase in hand.

"Your father plans to be home right after he shows a house in Woodstock."

"Okay."

"He's been pretty good lately," she added, patting me on the back. I smiled.

My mother started the station wagon then pulled away from the curb and up Depot Avenue. Cabot's appliance store was dark, as was M'Lord and Lady's Hair Salon, where my mother had her hair done. Everyone was home celebrating Thanksgiving, a big event in this small Vermont town.

"Your father will be happy to see you." We drove up Lowell Street and turned left into the parking lot, stopping in front of the big yellow barn opposite the house. My great grandfather had stored his collection of antique cars in the left side and stabled his carriage horses in the right.

The kitchen smelled of turkey. My mother's vegetable and potato casseroles lined the counter, and a huge bowl of iceberg lettuce sat on the drop leaf table waiting to get dressed. On the island *Mastering the Art of French Cooking* was opened to turkey gravy.

I gazed around the familiar kitchen, my eyes landing on the red Formica counter tops, scratched and stained. The vintage kitchen had seen better days, but my mother handled its quirks with remarkable ease. She knew how to adjust the sink faucet, as well as when to call David Reynolds if a leak persisted. The refrigerator door didn't always shut, so my mother always gave it that second push just in case. She moved around her space like a conductor, spoon in hand, directing traffic.

The front door opened. "Frederica, it's good to see you. How was the trip?" My father gave me a hug, kissed me on the cheek, and put his briefcase down.

"Fine."

"Good." He looked at me. "Exams?"

"I think they went well." *Except for Latin*, I thought. He touched my arm.

"I hope so," said my father. "You look well, Frederica."

"Thanks." I leaned against the counter, feeling its rough edge. My father removed his coat and hung it up, placing his Irish tweed hat on the shelf above the rack. It reminded me of the many hours my father and I spent at the barn mucking out and cleaning tack. That hat rarely left my father's head.

"Helen," he said to my mother, "you'd like the Corcorans, a damned attractive couple from Connecticut. I hope they buy the house."

"Which house is it?"

"The Dexter's guesthouse, which comes with a large parcel of land and a small barn. The Corcorans have horses."

He walked into the living room, and I heard the clink of ice against glass. Jim Beam with a dash of bitters and a little water. The liquor cabinet, an old pine chest with lopsided doors in the front, stood next to the worn-out Steinway piano my mother had inherited from her grandfather. Some of the thin, ivory pieces were cracked, a few missing.

An old oriental, also inherited, covered most of the living room floor. A large dark spot under the piano was Button's favorite pee spot. A fan, always on, tried to reduce the pungent smell that permeated through the room. My mother's dog ruled the house; urinating on the rug was one of his pleasures.

My father returned to the kitchen. "Good to be home. I've had a long day." He took a sip from his glass.

Upstairs we could hear footsteps along the hall and water running.

"Helen," my father asked, looking up, "has Sherman arrived?"

"Yes, and the others, as well. They parked in back."

"Good." He returned to the living room.

I left the kitchen and carried my bag to my bedroom on the second floor. I sat on the bed and stared at the wallpaper my mother had chosen, pale blue with dusty pink flowers strung together by long, winding, olive green stems. The window shades were open, and I could see the weathervane on the top of the yellow barn and the holes made by my brother Nick's BB gun. He was a good shot. I was disappointed when I heard he wouldn't be home this Thanksgiving. And my sister was spending a few days at a friend's house. I was on my own.

I shifted my gaze to the yellow bookshelf; on the top, two black ceramic horse heads stared at each other. Horse books filled the first shelf, many given to me by my father. *Misty of Chincoteague* and *The Black Stallion*, my favorites. Thornton W. Burgess and Beatrix Potter books lined the second shelf. How I loved *Old Mother West Wind* and *Adventures of Reddy Fox*. And Peter Rabbit? How could I forget him? The bottom shelf held a few Bobbsey Twins books.

I unpacked my suitcase, lined up the three pairs of shoes on the closet floor, and hung up my skirt, blouses, and new dress, which I would wear tonight. It fit pretty well but was a little snug around my waist. I sat down at the dressing table and looked into the mirror, stretching my mouth into a smile.

I picked up my comb and tried to make sense out of my long brown hair, always a chore. Sometimes I braided it, sometimes I pulled it into a ponytail, and sometimes I let it just hang, tucked behind my ears. Tonight, I would let it hang. I took my new dress out of the closet and laid it on the bed. Its vertical purple and green stripes would, I hoped, remove a few unwanted pounds.

Voices and laughter drifted up the stairs. The party had begun. I pulled the dress over my head, zipped up the back, and buckled the black leather belt, noticing I didn't have to let it out. Pleased, I chose the low black heels to complement the belt. A strand of pearls and pearl drop earrings finished the outfit. One last peek in the mirror. I pushed back a few unruly strands of hair and headed for the stairs.

I was turning left into the living room when Uncle Billy approach me.

"Hello, Freddy." He bent over and kissed my check. "Home until Sunday?" I nodded. As Uncle Billy walked toward the kitchen, my father appeared in his black velvet slippers embroidered with golden fox heads, yellow moleskin vest, and scarlet hunting tailcoat. His stomach strained against the buttons, but somehow they stayed fastened. On the lapel was his hunt insignia with the initials W.W.F.H., West Windsor Fox Hunt. My father and a friend, Pete Brooks, started the hunt about eight years ago.

"Frederica, you look wonderful." My father's eyes caught mine.

"Thanks," I murmured. He took my arm and steered me into the living room, where we stopped to talk with Henk, a top dressage rider from Holland who had immigrated to the States about fifteen years ago.

"Frederica, good to see you," said Henk. "Have you been riding?"

"Not much," I said, adding that school took up a lot of time.

"Yes, of course." Henk smiled.

"We'll be hunting tomorrow," my father said. "Join us?"

Henk declined, of course. My father's hunt didn't suit this meticulous, old-school rider. My father nodded and turned toward the bar.

I wandered into the kitchen. My mother, wearing her blue apron, was adding flour to the turkey drippings. "Can I help?" Yes, I could. I measured a second tablespoon of flour, adding it to the pan. "A little water, please," said my mother. I filled a cup with water and slowly poured it into the pan as my mother stirred. Soon, the mixture thickened. My mother turned off the heat and left the pan on the stove.

"Come, Freddy, let's join the others."

A plate of Vermont cheddar cheese and Ritz crackers sat on the cribbage board bench in front of the fire. I sat down and cut a piece of cheese from the huge chunk and placed it on a cracker. One would be okay.

I flattened my hands against the hard bench, letting my fingers dance on the wood. I remembered when my father waltzed with me at his aunt's eightieth birthday party a year ago. He was a good dancer. I had worn a dark red dress, one of my favorites. My father had commented on it.

I stood up and headed for the downstairs bathroom and locked the door. I looked into the mirror and removed a tiny scab from my left cheek. My mother's row of lipsticks sat on the shelf above the sink, offering a wide range of shades. Wine Red? Nope, a lighter one would be better. I rubbed the dark lipstick off and applied Scarlett. The image in the mirror smiled back; I had chosen the right color.

I left the bathroom and stared at the huge print of a monkey that hung on the wall opposite the front door. Clutching a half-peeled yellow banana in its hand, the monkey's sly look caught my eye, as it always did.

"Dinner!" My mother stood in the living room door with her hands in the air, one holding her wooden spoon. The turkey and side dishes and gravy were waiting on the sideboard.

Toasts, cigars, and singing followed dinner with the usual assortment of Thanksgiving pies. After dinner, my father recited Shakespeare and sang "The Tattooed Lady," followed by Sherman's rendition of "My Last Cigar." Then Uncle Billy stood up, erect as a board, and sang his signature song, "Blood on the Saddle." When the brandy appeared after dinner, I slipped away.

The study was a peaceful oasis with bookshelves, a fireplace, couch, and two captain's chairs. I sat on the couch and stared straight ahead. The small television, the only one in the house, sat on a table behind the study door. Its bent rabbit ears fell sideways. Should I turn it on? Maybe not. Instead, I pulled out one of the six tattered family photo albums from the bookshelves and returned to the couch. My brother Nicky learning to ski. Me on a sled. Little Connie in her playpen. Skiing at Mont-Tremblant. Swimming at the pond.

I wandered into the kitchen and noticed all the empty bottles of wine that filled the sink and a spinach casserole on the island that my mother must have forgotten to serve. Or maybe she was saving it for tomorrow's brunch, another grand affair that following the annual Thanksgiving West Windsor fox hunt. I went upstairs and lay on my bed, staring at the ceiling light. One of the bulbs had burned out. My father would fix it tomorrow.

On Sunday, my mother dropped me off at the station at noon. I boarded the train, found a seat by myself, looked out the window, and watched my mother drive away. I sat quietly, hands in my lap. I stretched out my fingers and counted them. Ten! Lucky me.

I pushed my suitcase under the seat and opened the small white canvas bag. Inside was a tuna fish sandwich, an apple, and some cheddar cheese. In three hours, I'd be back at school.

Until Next Year

"Duck!" Nick yelled. I leaned forward on Miss Chance's neck to avoid the top of the door frame. She and I followed my brother into the dining room, past the long walnut table, and into the living room. Hoots from everyone greeted us as we came to a halt between the couch and the two chairs that flanked the stone fireplace. It was just after eleven thirty on New Year's Eve.

I smiled broadly, well aware of the impression this huge 16.2-hand horse made, standing quietly on the large, worn oriental rug, allowing everyone to pat her neck and rump.

"A beauty!" shouted Uncle Sherman, affectionately called Kiss Cuz, as he raised his glass. Uncle Sherman never worked a day in his life; instead, he polished the doorknobs on the Unitarian Church in Winchester, Massachusetts. An outdated but charming bachelor, Kiss Cuz came to all my parents' parties; he arranged the flowers and sang his favorite song, "My Last Cigar," while smoking his after-dinner Arturo Fuenco cigar. Everyone loved him. And why not? He was lovable, though somewhat useless, but nobody seemed to mind. Once he had tried to seduce my mother's best friend at her friend's request. "Hen," Sherman admitted to my mother, "I've tried in the morning, I've tried in the afternoon, and I've tried at night, and I just can't do it!" My mother's friend finally gave up and later married my mother's brother, also useless, but at least his unearned income was a tad bigger than Uncle Sherman's.

"Yes, she sure is," Uncle Billy echoed. Billy and his wife Sylvia were also constants at my parents' parties. Both Kiss Cuz and Uncle Billy were riders and had every right to admire my beautiful, bay, thoroughbred mare, who—I'm sure —wondered who the two loud and slightly inebriated older men were. She should have known because she'd seen them in the living room for the past two years!

"Frederica, well done," my father said as he took a swig of bourbon. All three men were dressed in hunting attire. My father wore his black velvet slippers with a fox head embroidered on each. He loved those darn things and wore them whenever he had the chance.

This family tradition began when I was eight years old and pony crazy. The first midnight, New Year's, living-room arrival was Honey, my darling black-and-white Shetland pony. That was the first time I was allowed to stay up and participate in what was to become a yearly event. My father had led Honey through the front door of our house, gave me a leg up, and the three of us strode triumphantly into the living room. I was thrilled. All that attention directed at me and my pony!

As I grew older, Bumblebee replaced Honey, Nosey replaced Bumblebee, Miss Chance replaced Nosey, and Cookie replaced Miss Chance. I was now sixteen and not as thrilled as I had been, even though—for the first fifteen minutes of so after my arrival—I soaked up the admiration and ohs and ahs from my parents' friends, whose enthusiasm was catching.

"Who's next?" My father looked round the room as I slid off Miss Chance and stood by her head.

"Me!" Sylvia beamed and put her hand on my father's arm.

"Here." My father laughed. "I'll give you a leg up." Sylvia, known for her always-first-and-ready-for-anything attitude, gamely and willingly lifted her skirt, and placed her left foot, now shoeless, on my father's hands.

"Up you go." And up she went, lifting her right leg up and over, swirling her purple silky skirt over Miss Chance's hind quarters. She waved her right hand around, leaned back, and took a deep breath.

"Oh, how wonderful!" Sylvia smiled at my father. "Roger, my glass!" Her Native American turquoise necklace bounced between her breasts as she looked left and then right. Miss Chance stood patiently during Silvia's performance, probably thinking, "I've been here before."

My mother had a turn, followed by Hilda and Sarah and Ann. The clock finally struck midnight, and everyone cheered wildly. "Happy New Year" ricocheted off the walls, and everyone kissed everyone else, including me.

At last, the show was over, and I led Miss Chance back through the dining room and kitchen, out the front door, and headed for the barn.

I gave Miss Chance an extra slice of hay and refilled her water bucket and wished her Happy New Year. I swear she smiled, a knowing smile, and I smiled back.

I gave her one more pat on the neck and whispered in her ear, "Until next year!"

The Horse Girl

What fun my two siblings and I had growing up, never for a moment thinking that we might be broke. We had everything we wanted. Horses, tennis court, large pond with dock and canoes, ski trips, pickup hockey games, winter cookouts, long weekend and holiday parties. Who were we? One of the town's three "prominent" families, at least that was what I thought.

Our household was the center of activity, and my parents' hospitality extended to everyone. Friends admired their energy and seemingly effortless ability to organize activities, inside and out. The Mahers' was the place to be.

Dinner parties with endless toasts and cigars and singing were part of my parents' long weekend house parties. Morning Bloody Marys followed by eggs Benedict breakfasts followed by a set or two of tennis followed by drinks and a one-thirty poached-salmon lunch. After a brief nap, some joined my father for a two-hour ride cross-country while others went for a swim. Everyone changed for dinner. After an hour or two of cocktails, my mother served a sumptuous roast-beef meal with potatoes, carrots and onions, and a few casseroles. No dessert except for Thanksgiving and Christmas. My parents didn't believe in desserts. Frequently looped, they retired to bed either during or right after dinner, but the party continued. Somehow the dishes got done.

My mother's small inheritance plus my father's meager salary kept us afloat, barely. From time to time, my mother had to borrow one thousand dollars from a close friend or five thousand dollars from her wealthy sister in Canada. As far as I knew, my mother didn't mind this indignity. I guess it was all part and parcel of their lifestyle. My father was known as the country squire, a role he cherished, and my mother as the ultimate hostess, a role she loved.

Horses loomed large in my family despite the financial hardship they caused. How my parents managed to keep six or seven horses at a time amazed me once I discovered they lived on credit.

Tom, who shod our horses, never expected to be paid on time. Instead, two whiskeys, some funny stories, and a slap on the back sufficed and bought my father more time. He was the inveterate charmer—my father that is.

John Robinson, our vet, and his wife played bridge with my parents. My father sang his praises to his horsey friends, so John was beholden to him for his expanding business.

"John," my father said, "I just gave your name to the Parkers; they moved here last month with their five horses."

"Thanks, Roger. I'm sure I'll hear from them."

And on it went. The more business John got from my father, the longer he was willing to wait for the check.

My parents charged everything, and the various shops in the small Vermont town where we lived were patient. Everyone loved my parents, so what is the big deal? Yes, they owed money, but in time they'd pay it back. "The check's in the mail."

But things suddenly changed. I was seventeen and home from boarding school, looking forward to a long weekend. I had just returned from a beautiful October ride and was heading for the barn. I saw my father waiting for me.

"How was your ride?"

"Wonderful!"

He cast a sideways glance at me as I unsaddled Candle Glow, a thoroughbred my father bought from a friend a few years ago.

"Frederica, some changes have to be made." He paused then said, "We have to cut down."

"Cut down?" I loosened Candle Glow's girth and shortened the stirrup leathers. "What do you mean?"

My father patted Candle Glow's neck and looked away. "Well, for a starter, no Columbus Day house party this year."

I started walking toward the barn leading Candle Glow, my father following. "And," he said, "we have to do something about the horses. It's just too much for your mother and me."

I glanced at him. "You mean sell the horses?"

"Not an easy thing to do," he said. We reached the barn, and I replaced the bridle with a halter and cross-tied Candle Glow; I removed the saddle and placed it on the saddle stand in the tack room. After sponging her down, I checked her feet and let her go. She rolled in the barnyard, stood up, shook herself off, and galloped to the upper field.

"What about the tack?" I had returned to the tack room, where my father was sitting in one of the two wicker chairs. I sat in the other one.

"Well, we'll sell most of it," he said. I gazed around the room; saddles sat on racks along the long wall, girths slung over them. Bridles hung on red hooks that I'd carefully screwed into the wall between the saddles. My eyes rested on the old, chipped, yellow bureau that held extra reins, bridle parts, bits, halters, spurs, leathers; a whole collection of tack was organized in those four drawers. The saddle stand in the middle of the tack room held saddle soap, sponges, scrapers, and three hoof picks. Liniment, Hooflex, pine tar, absorbine, and other horse-related products lived on the table under the windows.

Outside the tack room, halters and halter shanks dangled from a couple of huge spikes that my father had pounded into the partition between the tack room and the stalls. Horse blankets were draped over metal bars next to each stall.

"My saddle?" My father smiled. "You can keep it." That old Crosby saddle had seen a lot of action, and I would hate to part with it. I quickly cleaned it and returned it to its rack on the wall and looked up at all the ribbons I had won over the years that were pinned above the saddles and bridles.

I took a deep breath, smiled at my father, and nodded. "Well then, that's it."

"Yes, I'm afraid it is."

We closed the tack room door and climbed the steep steps to the top of the barn. My father paused. He'd sell the hay, he said, and the horse trailer. He knew a woman who was interested in both. And she'd give him a good deal.

I followed him out of the barn door and looked up the long pasture where the horses were grazing. Candle Glow lifted her head, pricked up her ears, then resumed eating.

Back at school, I put all my horse photos in the bottom drawer, gently tucking them under my sweaters. I looked into the mirror and said goodbye to the horse girl. But at least she had her saddle.

A few years later, however, my parents' finances improved, and everything returned to "normal." Horses filled the barn again, house parties resumed, my father returned to his role as country squire, and my mother as the ultimate hostess.

It was a good thing I kept my saddle! The horse girl had returned.

BLOODED

I searched the horizon, waving frantically. The huge ocean liner pulled away from Montreal, and I wondered when I'd see my parents again. I looked down at the water and watched the whitecaps rise and fall, brushing my hair back from my face. The wind hissed, and I covered my eyes with my hands, feeling the tears slowly find their way down my cheeks.

"Are you alright?"

"Yes," I responded to the kind lady who stood beside me.

"Are you traveling alone?"

"Yes," I replied, wiping my tears away. It was late September, 1957. I was 19 and on my way to Tuam, County Galway, Ireland, to work for Lady Molly Cusack-Smith, who hunted her own pack of hounds, The Birmingham and North Galway Hunt. It had all sounded terribly romantic, but now I wasn't so sure. After four years at a girls' boarding school, I was ready for adventure. College could wait, so here I was, all alone sailing across the Atlantic.

The kind lady patted me on the shoulder and moved away. I leaned against the rail and faced the wind. Its coldness slapped my face, but it felt good. I studied my right hand and moved the turquoise ring back and forth. A gift from my father, it never left my finger.

"So exciting," my friend Barbara said, who—with her mother—was at my "leaving-for-Ireland party." Barbara's mother's friend Margaret knew Lady Molly Cusack-Smith and had made the arrangements.

"She's a formidable woman with a sharp tongue, but an accomplished horseman. Frederica will have a splendid time there. Molly and Sir Dermot Cusack-Smith are divorced, but he visits from time to time." Margaret added that they have one child, Oonagh-Mary, who would be about ten and lived with Molly.

Molly took in paying guests to supplement her income, and the girls she "hired," including me, worked for room and board only and usually stayed for one hunting season, sometimes two.

My father had beamed. His horsey daughter having a chance to live and hunt in Ireland; what could be better? Vicarious pleasure indeed! His Irish heritage and love for hunting finally coming to fruition.

"Frederica, ride well and work hard," he said.

I packed my Crosby saddle and black riding boots in a huge trunk, surrounding them with clothes. I tucked in my velvet hunting helmet, which I filled with sox to save room, and finally placed my engraved hunting whip and horn on top. The lid closed easily.

Margaret advised me to have the local tailor in Tuam make me a black wool hunting jacket and two pairs of breeches. "He's cheap and good," she said. I decided to follow her advice.

...

Lady Molly met me at the dock.

"Over here!" She held the "Frederica" sign high in the air.

She stood upright, both feet planted solidly on the ground, sturdy brown brogues pointing straight ahead. I walked toward her.

"Hello," she said. "How was your voyage?"

She wore a green tweed skirt and olive Barber jacket, zipped shut. A silk scarf was tied in front, its ends tucked into the jacket. Her short greying hair, slightly wavy, framed her stern face.

"Fine." We found my luggage, which a porter put into the trunk of her Jaguar.

"I need to buy a bottle of gin. Come with me."

Five minutes later, I managed to drop that bottle of gin. "Bloody hell! What happened? Now I'll have to buy another." I was royally chastised.

I trailed along behind her, wondering what on Earth I was doing in this strange country with this overpowering, terrifying woman. But no turning back.

...

Molly drove, cursing at cars that were either too fast or too slow. "Frederica, see how they drive here?"

I nodded, hands folded in my lap. The trip was long and silent.

We finally arrived and followed the long, winding, tree-lined entrance to

Birmingham House, a large, square, pink Georgian house surrounded by acres of pastures, fields, and woodlands. Horses were grazing in the pastures that bordered the driveway.

Molly parked in front of the house. "Dick!" she yelled. "I need you, now. And where is Josey?"

A short man of about fifty appeared from behind the house. His long woolen overcoat, which I later learned he always wore, stopped just above his ankles. Dick Tighe managed the place and was one of three people who dared talk back to Molly. The others were May the cook, and Frank Gordon, an old friend and loyal hunt follower.

"Here I am." Josey, the hunt whip, appeared wearing grey, corduroy pants and a red and green plaid shirt. His cap tilted to one side, but that never seemed to matter; it never fell off. He had ruddy cheeks and light brown hair, which was neatly trimmed. He nodded to me, a huge smile spreading across his face. He and Dick lugged the trunk inside.

"Upstairs," Molly hollered. "The corner room at the end on the right." She led me through the entrance hall. I looked up at the light blue ceiling then down at marble-veined tiles that covered the floor. A table was placed to the left of the formal, wide staircase at the end of the room. *Cold and austere*, I thought. What a way to greet visitors.

"Follow me," Molly said. Upstairs we went, following Dick and Josey. A large, threadbare oriental rug covered the landing, and a few hunt scenes hung on the walls. Dick and Josey led me into my bedroom at the end of the landing on the right. It was furnished with two single beds, a dark inlaid dressing table, two chipped Chippendale chairs, and an old armoire with two drawers at the bottom. A puffy, dark-red comforter covered one of the beds.

"Unpack, then come downstairs." Molly's slightly arched eyebrows, perched on green eyes that bore right through me, moved upward as she barked out orders.

"Yes, alright," I said. "I will. Thanks." I didn't quite know why I was thanking her, but thanking her seemed like the right thing to do.

I hung my two dresses and three skirts in the armoire, carefully placing my riding boots, two pairs of shoes, and one pair of sneakers on the armoire floor. One of the two drawers had plenty of room for dungarees, shorts, and sweaters. The other held everything else. Pleased, I left my room and poked around. Five more bedrooms and four bathrooms completed the second floor. I picked up my saddle and wandered downstairs.

"Dick, take that to the tack room," Molly said.

"Yes," he said with a grin.

Molly walked me around the house. The living room had two couches opposite each other and two chairs that faced the fireplace. Paintings and a mirror hung on the mustard-colored walls; a blue-and-red oriental covered much of the floor.

The dining room was quite regal, I thought. A grand piano stood in a corner with an elaborate candlestick on top. "English nineteenth century sterling silver, been in my family for generations."

Molly then pointed to the gold-framed portraits that hung from each of the four dark-red walls. "That's John Dennis, my ancestor, and that one is me. The others are past owners of Birmingham House." I looked at each and nodded.

Four birch logs sat in the marble fireplace. Would she have a fire lit? I doubted it.

"The table seats twelve people. We will eat here every night, and we dress for dinner," said Molly.

Oh God, I thought, *dress for dinner? Margaret hadn't warned me.*

"And this is the smoking room." A deer head hung from the far orange wall, surrounded by prints of horses. Two well-worn couches flanked the fireplace. Oh, I guessed, this is where a fire would be lit. At least I hoped so. A standing lamp leaned precariously to one side.

"Now into the kitchen." I followed.

A small, grey-haired woman, wearing a dark blue apron, turned around. "May has been with me for years."

"Welcome," May said, then she returned to the sink. I noticed the huge stove. "An AGA cooker," Molly said.

What on Earth was an AGA cooker?

"Follow me." We walked out the back kitchen door into a large courtyard.

"We have sixteen box stalls; Dan, my kennelman, lives above those corner stalls." She added that the kennels were behind the yard, out of sight. Dan fed the hounds dead carcasses he collected from nearby farms. Like Dick Tighe, he'd been with her for years. He suddenly appeared out of his doorway, with a slightly crooked smile.

"Dan," Molly said, "this is Frederica, our new girl."

"Hello. Nice to meet you." He was a skinny fellow, toothless with a stubby beard and pasted-down hair, parted in the middle. I don't believe Dan changed his pants or shirt once in the two years I lived there. Suspenders kept his pants in place, but he also wore a brown leather belt.

"Come," Molly said. "I'll show you the horses."

We walked from stall to stall. "Friar's Joke; this one's Dusty." She stopped at the third stall and peered in. "Dick, where the hell is Firefox?"

"At the forge."

"And Tom Dooley?"

"Also at the forge."

Molly nodded then continued to walk from stall to stall, naming the different horses. "Finn, Rover, Misty, Danbury, Mercury. She stopped at Mercury's stall. "This is the horse I ride." Molly patted Mercury's large head. She continued on. "This one is Cob, your horse." I peered into the stall and watched Cob munching hay. He was about 15.2 hands high with a white stripe down his face. "These remaining stalls are for the young horses that we bring in at night."

I soon settled into a routine that Molly choreographed with an iron fist. Nobody questioned her decisions except Dick Tighe, May, and Frank Gordon.

I met Oonagh-Mary later that day. She was a shy, retiring girl who seemed terrified of her mother, and I soon discovered why. Molly rarely complemented her daughter but found a myriad of reasons to criticize her.

Oonagh-Mary ate in the kitchen, and Molly and I ate alone in the dining room, sitting on opposite ends of the long table, staring at each other through the arms of two majestic candleabras. Molly paid most of her attention to her dogs, which relieved me of trying to make conversation.

"Here!" Molly yelled to her four fox terriers, who yapped and jumped around at her feet, waiting for Molly to throw them pieces of her roast beef. "Jasper, this isn't for you!" Molly whacked Jasper, who whimpered and backed off. "Come, Rosey, eat up."

...

The first paying guests, Gerald and Ann Smith and William and Eliza Warren, arrived in mid-October. And pay they did. "I need the money," Molly told me. "How else can I keep this place going?" Dinners were elegant but modest, and Molly's ample garden and root cellar supplied vegetables throughout the year. But she did have to buy meat, chicken, and fish.

"One chicken thigh per person," she told May. "And cover each with plenty of mushroom sauce," which camouflaged the portion size. "Tonight, cocktails at five thirty. Dinner at six thirty sharp."

Tomorrow was Saturday, the first hunt of the season and my first Irish hunt. I was excited! We were to meet at Ryan's Pub in Athenry, not far from Tuam.

I woke at seven o'clock, dressed quickly, and joined the others for one of

May's delicious breakfasts. Fresh eggs and bacon from a local farmer, plus May's warm, just-out-of-the-oven bread, which we plastered with homemade butter and jam. Molly poured hot coffee into mugs and passed these around.

At eight thirty the action began. I met Josey in the yard, and we tacked up the horses, loaded three into the horse box. Josey and I rode two and led the others five miles to Ryan's Pub. Dick drove the horse box, and Molly the trailer with the hounds. It was grey and cold; the mist hadn't cleared, and the hazy, damp air clung to our riding jackets.

"We hunt on Tuesday and Saturday from mid-October to early March," Josey said. "And our country spans just over thirty square miles, mostly limestone pastures and dry, sometimes-crumbling stone walls. Some are high, but our horses are great leppers." Leppers? I'd never heard that word before. But Josey's Irish accent gave it meaning. "Cob," Josey said, "can get over anything." I couldn't wait.

We arrived at the pub around ten thirty. Horses were being unloaded and tacked up. Dick held Molly's horse as she stood on the horse box ramp and mounted Mercury. Dick tightened the girth and checked Molly's stirrup leathers. "All set," he said. Fifteen or so riders made up the field, each a loyal follower of Molly's hunt. These included Anita and Bill King, Lord Peter Patrick and Lady Ann Hemphill, and Mrs. Drury, who sat perched on her big grey horse. I noticed a leather strap around her horse's neck, which I soon learned she held on to for dear life. Another frequent participant was the local priest, Tom O'Flaherty. He was a jolly fellow who rode a huge, chestnut, Irish draft horse named Stout who had big round feet. It seemed to me that his horse was as jolly as Tom himself. They made a wonderful pair, Stout galumphing across the fields like an elephant and Tom aboard with a huge smile on his face.

Frank Gordon rarely missed a hunt. He served as Master, and his son Henry often whipped in, along with Josey. Henry had premature grey hair and a chiseled face, piercing blue eyes, and a ready smile. He was a lady's man, which I quickly found out. A gifted horseman, he glided across country, effortlessly lifting his mount (it didn't seem to matter what horse he rode) over high gates and double walls, upward of four feet. I never saw his horse stumble once the entire two years I lived in Ireland.

Molly's hunt couldn't compare to the Galway Blazers, an established, successful, well-endowed hunt that attracted people from all over the world. But her hunt was a robust affair, even though the field was small.

I helped the paying guests mount their horses, checking girths and leathers, then climbed on Cob, a horse I soon learned had great courage and amazing jumping ability. No beauty, but he cleared obstacles with room to spare. After the riders had mounted, Dick walked from rider to rider, collecting the capping fee. And the pub owner followed with a tray of port, the traditional "stirrup cup" to give riders the courage they needed to navigate the difficult terrain and jump challenging obstacles.

Molly finished a second glass, and off we clattered down the macadam road. Josey and Henry whipped in, and Molly—dressed in her scarlet hunting coat— hunted the hounds and gave out the orders. The rest of us rode behind Frank Gordon and obediently waited at the first covert, watching the hounds sniffing, trying to find a scent. Molly encouraged the hounds to draw the covert, and we sat in silence, waiting to see what would happen.

Suddenly, we heard the excited cry of the hounds, followed by the staccato sound of Molly's horn signaling the fox had broken cover, had bolted. "GONE AWAY" Frank yelled, pointing in the direction that the fox had taken. Molly, Josey, and Henry took off, followed by Frank and the rest of us in hot pursuit. We raced through fields and jumped stone walls that crisscrossed the mostly open country. The hounds were in full cry. It was exciting!

Then things came to a standstill. After an hour of hard riding, the hounds had lost the scent. A check! Horses caught their breath, flasks came out, people smiled and nodded to each other, relaxing, but on edge, ready to go again. The hounds recovered the scent, and we were off and running. A half hour later, the fox went to ground.

"We have him now," Josey yelled at Dick, who had followed the hunt in Molly's car with the fox terriers. He arrived, terriers in hand, and encouraged them to scamper down the holes, forcing the fox to bolt, which, alas it did, only to end up in the jaws of the hounds.

"We've got him!" Josey yelled, and he grabbed the sad fox by its tail and waved it around, encouraging the crazed hounds to tear it to pieces, blood dripping from their jaws. Everyone cheered and yelled and clapped! Exciting! Tantalizing! I was in ecstacy. My first kill! After the frenzy stopped, Josey pasted blood on my cheek with part of the fox's carcass, what was left of it, and as I touched the blood, I knew I had paid my dues and had entered this primal world of Irish fox hunting.

Two years and many hunts later, I left Ireland with my Crosby saddle, my trunk, and many memories. I had survived eighty-eight hunts with the Birmingham and North Galway Hunt, nine with the Galway Blazers, and four with the Tipperary Hunt. This experience was living proof that the world of Somerville and Ross was not yet dead in Ireland.

I know that my father would agree, especially when he sang, off key, his rendition of "If You Ever Go Across the Sea to Ireland." Never a stickler for correct lyrics, he sang with gusto and nostalgia.

After all, his horsey daughter had been "blooded" in Co. Galway! What could be better than that?

My father in his cavalry uniform, 1944.

My father jumping a wall in a cavalry event at Fort Riley, Kansas, 1944.

My father on Big Mare competing in the Woodstock, Vermont, 100 Mile Ride, 1947.

My father holding my sister Connie, my mother, my brother Nick, and me. Photo from our 1947 Christmas card.

I'm riding Nosey competing in the Woodstock, Vermont, 100 Mile Ride, 1948.

My father leading Nosey, with my mother and me, returning to the barn after finishing the first day of the Woodstock, Vermont, 100 Mile Ride, 1948.

My mother on Martial Maid competing in the Woodstock, Vermont, 100 Mile Ride, 1948.

Nosey and I won the 100 Mile Junior Division—I believe in 1950.

I'm riding Martial Maid in an equitation class.

Pete Brooks on Spunky, 1953.

November, 1953, South Woodstock—Sheddsville hill. My father, Pete Brooks, and a few friends at an early morning meet of the West Windsor Fox Hunt.

Martial Maid and I jumping a post and rail fence at a horse show.

Miss Chance and I jumping the outside course at a horse show.

Miss Chance and I jumping the outside course in a Vermont horse show.

FREDERICKA MAHER, a Windsor Lion's Club Horse show winner last year in the knock-down-and-out jumping class, on Miss Chance, hopes to repeat her victory in the 5th annual Windsor Lion show coming up on the week end at Buena Vista Farms. There have been 70 horses and 210 entries so far registered and horses are

Newspaper clipping. I'm on Miss Chance competing in a knock down and out class.

I'm on Nosey and my father on Martial Maid; we're competing in the Woodstock, Vermont, 100 Mile Ride, 1953.

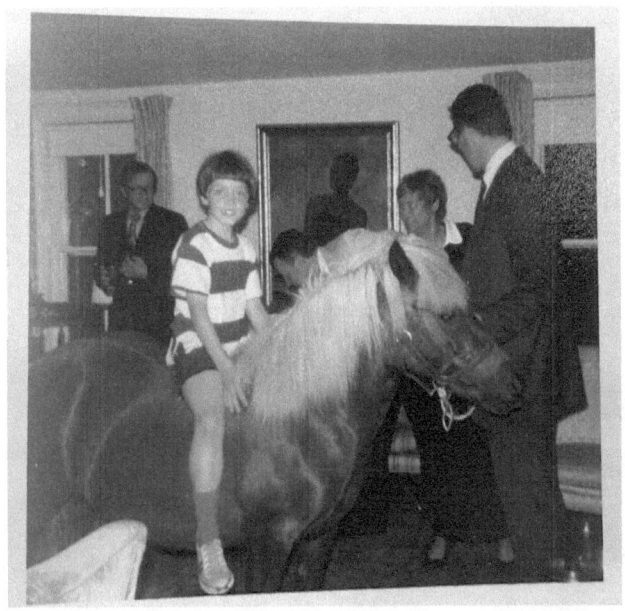

Son Daniel on our pony in our living room. An annual New Year's Eve event! My brother Nick is holding Cookie, and cousin Hollis Smith is in the background.

I'm on Chance Son in the Woodstock, Vermont, 100 Mile Ride, 1972.

The horse barn burned down in 1972, and here I am sifting through the burned debris searching for the metal medallions of horse show ribbons I'd won over the years.

Arthur on Zelda.

My father on Prompted, 1982.

I'm riding Prompted in Brownsville, Vermont. Taken by my father. We were on our way to a beautiful high spot for a picnic lunch. 1981.

On Prompted riding with a friend in Brownsville, Vermont, 1982

I'm riding Harry in the Susan G. Komen Ride for the Cure in Woodstock, Vermont. I believe this was in 2013 or 2014.

Fox-Hunting Heaven

New Year's day was particularly cold that year.

Just up the unplowed and slippery road above John Howland's house, Pete's riderless horse Spunky caught up with us.

This old, reliable, black horse with an ugly head and great temperament always carried Pete safely across the country. Not overly graceful, both horse and rider complemented each other. Today something had happened, and we were pretty sure it wasn't Spunky's fault.

We stopped, dismounted, caught Pete's horse, and looked around. Where was Pete?

"There!" My father pointed to Pete, who was lying on the road maybe 200 feet below us.

Ten years ago, my father and Pete Brooks founded the West Windsor Fox Hunt. They bought Star Dust, a young well-bred hound, from Betty Fields, friend and joint master of the Nashoba Valley Fox Hunt in Massachusetts. Gradually, the pack grew to twelve couples, or twenty-four in all. They were kenneled at Pete's place, a small farm at the end of a dirt road.

The field was a motley crew at best; anyone in the least bit interested joined the fun—young, old, experienced, inexperienced. Everyone was welcome. After all, the dues for membership helped keep the hunt alive. On good days, maybe sixteen people showed up. Today, however, our tiny group consisted of my father, Pete, my brother Nick, and me. Fox hunting on New Year's day had become a tradition, and we went out no matter how many people participated.

We quickly led the horses down to road. Pete was on his back, one arm tucked under him, the other nestled by his side. His eyes were closed, but his mouth was half-open.

"Is he alive?" I looked at Nick.

"I don't know."

"Maybe he is," my father said. He removed his heavy sheepskin coat and gently laid it over Peter. "To keep him warm."

Nick added his warm jacket, tucking it under Pete's back. I did the same.

"To keep him warm," my father repeated as he remounted his horse. "I have to get to a phone."

He rode down the road to the nearest house, not far. Nick and I held the horses, waiting. We could hear the hounds baying in the distance. Were they chasing a fox or a deer?

Turning to me, Nick said, "Freddy, I don't think he's alive." I nodded. Snow had begun to fall as I leaned over Pete searching for signs of life.

Twenty minutes later, my father returned. "An ambulance is coming. How's Pete?" He dismounted and gave his horse to me to hold. "Is he breathing?"

"I don't think so," Nick said. I watched as my father placed his hand on Pete's neck, then pushed the snow away from Pete's head.

"That's better," my father said. He stood up and searched the road, looking for the ambulance. "I wish they'd hurry."

"There it is," Nick said, pointing down the road. The ambulance, slipping and sliding, came to a stop. The driver and a second man walked the rest of the way, holding a stretcher.

"We were lucky to get as far as we did. I'm Dave, and this is Michael. What happened?"

"He fell off his horse, without any warning," my father said. "Is he alive?"

Dave bent over and looked at Peter. "I don't think so," he said. "But we need to hurry." Michael helped Dave gently slide Pete onto the stretcher. Dave gave us our coats and covered Pete with two blankets.

"Be careful," my father said, looking straight at Dave.

"We will. Can someone help us carry the stretcher?"

"Nick?" My father nodded at my brother.

Nick, Dave, and Michael carried Pete down the slick road to the waiting ambulance. My father and I watched, holding the four horses, as the ambulance disappeared down the road.

"Frederica," my father said. "Pete's a great guy. A great guy."

"Yes," I said. My father turned away and looked up the road toward

Sheddsville. He rubbed his hands, like he always did, and slid them into the huge pockets of his sheepskin coat. The snow continued to fall, adding inches to the road.

"Let's go," my father said as he remounted his horse leading Spunky down the road. Nick and I mounted and followed. Friends who lived nearby stabled the horses and drove us to the hospital.

"I'm sorry," the doctor said. "He had a heart attack, probably very sudden— He didn't feel anything."

We silently drove home, the windshield wipers working full-time because of the driving snow.

"Roger," my mother asked, "what did the doctor say?"

My father looked at her and shook his head. He hung up his sheepskin coat and walked into the living room. We heard ice cubes clinking against the side of a glass. Probably bourbon. With bitters. He reappeared in the kitchen, clutching his glass, already half empty.

"Jesus, a hell of a day." My father turned to look at me standing against the opposite counter. "Pete was a great guy," he said as he walked back into the living room, clutching his now-empty glass.

The hounds eventually made their way home, but Pete was not there to greet them. My father moved the hounds to a renovated shed near our house. The West Windsor Fox Hunt lasted another few years, then my father sold all the hounds except Sampler, his favorite. Sampler lived happily in the house for five more years. He was a great hound, and Pete was a great guy, and I'm sure they have reunited in that mysterious place called fox-hunting heaven.

Horse of a Lifetime

When my father returned from WWII in 1946 (he stayed an extra year in Okinawa), I was eight years old. The first thing he did was buy Big Mare, a 16.2-hand horse for himself, and two ponies, one for me and one for my ten-year-old brother. My fourteen-year-old Shetland pony, Honey, had a mind of her own. But she was obedient enough, and I rode her all over our property, bareback or with a saddle. When I turned ten, I began riding Big Mare, who was quiet and steady.

A year later, my father decided I needed a horse with more potential, so he bought a three-year-old thoroughbred off the track. Although she had two bowed tendons, she never took a lame step. We named her Miss Chance, and she lived a happy twenty-six years and was a talented mount, as well as a friendly stable mate to many other horses that passed through our barn.

When I turned twelve on June 2, 1950, my father decided both Miss Chance and I had potential. As a result, he hired Gaston Hammery, a dressage rider who had emigrated from Hungary after the war, to give me riding lessons 5 days a week all summer.

Slim, upright, and serious, Gaston Hammery cut a dashing figure, at least in my twelve-year-old eyes. He always wore polished brown riding boots and tan breeches, a tweed jacket, a blue shirt, and maroon silk scarf tied around his neck. And he carried a crop. My father always referred to him as "correct." I never quite knew what that meant.

My father had been in the cavalry, stationed at Fort Riley, Kansas, and all that order and neatness had left a strong impression on him. "Frederica, first impressions are important. Make sure your boots are clean and your hair is braided. And Miss Chance should be carefully groomed, and check her pasterns and between her front legs. Brush her tail and mane, as well." I dutifully followed his instructions.

Gaston Hammery's lessons were tough, but Miss Chance and I learned together under his sharp, watchful eyes. "Sit deeeep in the saddle; poosh, poosh, poosh; keeeep your hands steeeel." And so it went hour after hour, day after day, week after week. By the end of the summer, both Miss Chance and I had come a long way.

I remember feeling very special being taught by a real-life Olympic Hungarian dressage rider, whose strong accent added to his mystique. I was sure that both Miss Chance and I would improve because of his credentials, and I was right.

Miss Chance and I showed all over New England and sometimes in Canada, and we won our fair share of ribbons and trophies. I also evented her and rode her in competitive trail rides, as well as hunted her at various hunts in Massachusetts. After she retired, I rode her for pleasure. Throughout all these years, she was a willing companion, a courageous mount, a talented jumper, a steady horse mate to the other horses, and as reliable a horse as you could ever find.

When she turned twenty-six in 1972, I knew this would be her last birthday. Labored breathing, or heaving, had become noticeably worse over the summer months.

"Frederica, it's time to put Miss Chance down before cold weather sets in." My father turned to me then looked up at the horses grazing in the upper field.

It was five o'clock p.m., feeding time, and my father called to the horses. "Come here, come here." Miss Chance's ears perked up, and she led the pack down the field to the barn. This was just one of her many jobs. The other horses obediently followed her as she wound her way down on the path she had made years before. I could hear her heaving as she neared the barn.

After the horses finished eating, I let them out of their stalls, and they hung around the barn.

I patted Miss Chance's neck, gathered her mane, and led her to the stone wall near the pasture fence. I climbed on the wall and lifted my leg over her back and slid on. She stood there waiting for instructions. I gently squeezed her sides, and she walked slowly toward the gate. Did she think we were going for a trail ride? Maybe.

"Good girl," I said, patting her neck. "You're the best." She stopped at the gate, waiting for me to open it. Instead, I slid off her back and rubbed her face. "No trail ride today."

I looked into her kind eyes and walked away.

That October, Dan dug a huge hole in the pasture with his backhoe. I got in my car and drove away. Arthur, my husband, led Miss Chance to the hole and stood there, whispering in her ear, "Freddy says goodbye." John, our vet, stroked Miss Chance on her neck and quickly injected her with pentobarbital. She collapsed into the hole.

I parked in Sheddsville, high on a hill where I could see our property at a distance, tears streaming down my cheeks. "Miss Chance," I whispered, "you were my horse of a lifetime."

What's a Little Fire?

The phone rang. "Hello?"

"Freddy, the barn is burning down!" my mother yelled.

"What?"

"Come quickly!"

What was she talking about? "What happened?"

"Not sure, but hurry."

"Coming!" I put the phone down and called to my husband, Arthur, who was getting dressed.

"Arthur, the barn's on fire! I have no idea what happened, but I'm off."

"What? On fire?"

"Yes, I'm driving over." We were renting a house in Sheddsville for the summer, about two miles from my parents' house and barn. At this hour of the morning, the horses would be in their stalls having breakfast. Not a good situation.

"Feed the kids, okay?" Daniel and Alex were still sleep. It was just after six in the morning. I ran out the door, jumped into the car, and raced down the dirt road, driving well above the speed limit, whatever it was. But I figured people wouldn't be out at this time of day, so I was safe—as were they!

Smoke filled the air as I drove up Kimball Farm Road. My mother frantically waved to me as I approached. I parked on the side of the road and jumped out of the car. I stared at what was left of the barn, black smoke spewing out from burned debris.

"Oh my God, what happened? And where are the horses?"

"Your father saw the smoke, ran back down to the barn, which he'd just left—probably not more than a half hour after feeding the horses. Somehow, he got the horses out of their stalls. Hazen arrived in time to help him." Hazen, a neighbor, and my father had managed to herd the six horses into the lower pasture and close the gate. Horses often return to a burning barn.

The entire four-story barn had collapsed like a falling giant oak tree. I walked down the path to where my father and Hazen were standing.

"How did it start?"

"Don't know. Probably faulty wiring. Hazen, what do you think?"

"Yup, I imagine faulty wiring. Then the dry hay caught fire. An old barn like this would easily go up in flames." Hazen shook his head. "A pity. An old barn like this."

"Yes, a pity," my father said. In just a few minutes, everything was destroyed. Tack and other horse paraphernalia, tractor, jeep, truck, horse trailer, hay bales, random equipment. Thousands of dollars down the drain. The black smoke swirled up into the atmosphere, competing with the morning clouds. The smell was horrible, the heat unbearable. We left the scene and walked to my parents' house, entering through the kitchen door.

"Well," my father said, "what a disaster. We'll have to do something with the horses."

"Yes," I replied. I was training for the 100 Mile Ride in South Woodstock. My horse and the one Arthur was riding needed a roof over their heads and grain twice a day. Arthur wasn't competing, but he trained with me just the same. I would choose between Chance Son and Raven, selecting the one I thought would be ready and fit at just the right time. And now, where on Earth could we stable our two, plus the other four?

"The Reeves' place," my father interjected. "I know Stella would be happy to board both until the ride in September. You only have a few weeks to go."

I nodded. "A good solution. Will you call?" He would. A few hours later, it was settled. Our two horses would spend the rest of August at the Reeves' farm in South Woodstock, and Stella's groom Ernie would feed morning and night. Now what about the other horses?

"We'll figure out something," my father said. And he did. The remaining horses would be kept at our neighbor's upper pasture that had a run-in shed. This would suffice. My father would feed morning and night.

A few days later, when the ground had cooled and the charred machinery had been hauled away, I crawled around in the ashes, searching for all my hard-won horse show ribbons and trophies. Miraculously, some metal medallions and pieces of various trophies had survived.

A fire hadn't destroyed the memories, only the proof. I'd been there and done that, and that's all that mattered. What's a little fire?

A VALUABLE LESSON

"Arthur, let's go."

Arthur and I had tacked up our two horses, Chance Son and Raven, and were headed for the white birches. The year was 1973, and it was mid-August. I was thirty-five and determined to ride in the 100 Mile this year because my father owned two horses that were capable of competing. And who knew what the future would hold, so I decided this was the year.

Arthur learned to ride at camp when he was a kid, and although he knew that walking, trotting, and cantering in a ring did not prepare him for trail riding in Vermont, he was game. I made sure he was mounted on a sensible horse. Raven, although a thoroughbred, was just that horse. He had lots of experience and was rarely spooked.

"Beautiful day," I said, as we trotted along the dirt road past Stella and Lloyd Reeve's house. When my parents' barn burned down, we moved these two horses to the Reeves' barn. Lloyd and Stella were good friends, and they happily obliged. Their groom Ernie, a funny, older, and wizened guy from Florida (the Reeves wintered there), took good care of Chance Son and Raven. His accent was hilarious. "Y'all have a dandy ride" was his favorite line every time we left the barn.

I had about two more weeks to train for the 100 Mile Ride. Because horses covered forty miles in seven hours on the first and second days, and twenty miles in three hours on the third, I had to make sure Chance Son or Raven could cover the ground within the time allowed. Both horses were doing well, so I knew it could be a difficult choice when the time came.

Arthur and I rode another mile or so, turned left, and followed the trail—bordered by white birches—through the woods up a steep hill into an open field, where we always stopped to admire the 360-degree panorama. Today, we could see for miles.

"Gorgeous," I said.

"Yes, it is."

We sat quietly for a few minutes, enjoying the view. We called this spot "Top of the World," and top of the world it was. Now owned by a friend, she allowed horses and skiers to use her property.

"What a spot," he added. "No wonder your friend bought this property."

"Yes, I know."

We continued down through a pasture, weaving through junipers sprinkled here and there. At the bottom, we crossed the dirt road and entered the woods that would eventually lead to another open field.

Suddenly, without warning, a loud crash interrupted our peaceful ride. Raven spooked and took off down the narrow path.

"Hang on!" I yelled at Arthur as he was flying down the trail, totally out of control. I watched Raven gallop around the bend and disappear.

Oh oh, I thought to myself. *This looks bad.*

A few minutes later, I caught up with Arthur.

"Jesus, what could I do?" He patted Raven, who was standing quietly.

"Nothing." I replied. "Sometimes this happens. A tree fell somewhere. What a noise!"

Arthur nodded. "It's a miracle I stayed on."

"Well," I said, "you did, and that's the main thing." We laughed and continued down the trail.

After leaving the horses in the competent hands of Ernie, we drove home.

"Arthur, remember when Zelda arrived back at the barn without you?"

"Yup, I remember," he said, smiling. Zelda was kind of ugly, but she was solid and forgiving, or at least I thought she was. A polo-player friend of mine had retired her and was looking for a good home. I liked Zelda and thought she'd be a good horse for Arthur.

Arthur and Zelda had left the barn on a beautiful summer afternoon around two o'clock for a ride along the snowmobile trail that headed for the big meadow just below Mt. Ascutney. An hour later, Zelda returned without Arthur. I jumped on her back and galloped up the road in search of Arthur. He had just reached the dirt road and was strolling along.

"Hey, what happened?" I asked.

"Goddamn it, she dumped me."

"Why?"

"I don't know why," he said.

"Where?"

"Just at the top of the field."

I wondered if Zelda had been bitten by a bee—something had to have spooked her.

"Were you trotting or cantering?"

"Trotting just below the tree line."

"Hmm," I said, "maybe you weren't paying attention?"

Arthur smiled and said, "Maybe I wasn't."

Thanks, Zelda, for this valuable lesson. This time Arthur paid attention and stayed on!

Business Is Business

"Tom, I have another horse for you." I held the phone between my left shoulder and my ear, leaning against the wall in the feed room.

Tom was my pal; I'd known him since he was six or seven. His parents and my parents were close friends, so we sort of grew up together even though I was five years older.

"You do? What is it this time?"

"Not a bad one; I think you'll like him. I bought him last year from Lana Brown—actually from her husband—but she was the negotiator. He's a thoroughbred, about 16.2 hands and hunted in Virginia. He's ten, I think. No papers."

"Okay, what have you done with him?"

"Not much," I said, "other than trail-riding, mostly cross-country. He loves to jump and never refuses, which is a plus. Walls mostly, but once or twice gates and some post and rails."

"Name? Color?"

"Accolade. Kind of brown, but a darker brown," I said. "He's a nice-looking horse and sound."

Tom and I had an informal arrangement. I bought horses, rode them for a bit, then sent them to Tom, who worked them on the flat and then sold them. We split the proceeds. I tried to find bargains, horses that an owner needed to unload for various reasons, or a horse that had potential but the owner hadn't done much with it. Sometimes, I'd find retired polo horses or horses off the track. Tom and I had a good thing going for about ten years.

"Freddy, can I pick him up this Saturday?"

Today was Tuesday, and Saturday worked just fine. "Sure," I said. "Time?"

"Noon?"

"Perfect. See you then."

I put down the phone and wandered into the aisle. Accolade was standing quietly, enjoying the cool barn. It was mid-July and hot. The other horses were milling around, swatting flies with their tails. I walked up to Accolade and patted him on the neck.

"Well, I guess you'll be gone in a few days." I was sorry, really sorry, because I liked this horse a lot.

One last ride, I decided, before saying goodbye to Accolade. I cross-tied him, tacked him up, and led him to the mounting block. I mounted him, and off we went, up the pasture to the gate at the far end. He stood still while I opened the gate then closed it behind us.

We continued through the upper hay field, jumped the stone wall at the far end, and headed for the trailer. Yes, a trailer hunters used during deer season. It was a ratty old thing, rusty and dirty. We walked past it and up the steep wooded hill, picking our way along. Accolade was sure-footed and nothing seemed to bother him.

We reached the top and took a breather. It was hot. Accolade and I continued along the ridge to the familiar trail that wound down the other side.

Soon, we reached our neighbor's field that had once been a cow pasture, but now was overgrown. He had sold all his milk cows about fifteen years ago, including his heifers that he had once pastured here. Accolade carefully picked his way through the field, full of shrubs and rocks and fallen branches. At the bottom of the pasture, we turned left and headed for home.

I called Tom that evening. "Would you be upset if I kept Accolade a while longer?"

"How come?"

"Well, I like this horse, and it's only July. I'd love to enjoy him for another month at least."

"So are we talking August?"

I thought a moment then said, "Sure, August—late August?"

"You know," Tom said, "fall is a harder time to sell horses, and I need to school him a bit before selling him."

"I do know that," I said, "but Accolade also hunts, so that's a plus."

"Can I think about this?"

"Sure," I said.

A few days later, Tom called to say he'd split the difference. He had found a buyer who was really interested in Accolade and wanted him by the second week in August. Would that be okay with me? I wanted to tell him no, it wouldn't be okay with me, but I hesitated. "I'll let you know tomorrow, okay?"

My old mare, Miss Chance, had been gone for many years, and Accolade was the first horse that sort of replaced her. It's hard to find just the right horse, and when you do, it's harder to let go.

I called Tom the next day. "Tom, I don't suppose you'd reconsider and wait till the end of August?"

Silence.

"I know this is a lot to ask, especially because you have a buyer."

Tom was good at his business. One reason was that he kept his promises, was an honest horse guy—traits that some consider rare in horse-trading. Yes, he was a shrewd bargainer, astute but not cagey. He was well-respected.

"Freddy, I honestly don't think this will work."

"Oh, you don't?"

"No, not really. I've already told the buyer he'd have the horse mid-August, and he's willing to pay a good price—good for you and for me."

"Yes, I know. Give me a few more hours."

I meandered down to the barn, had a long look at Accolade, patted him on the shoulder, said goodbye, and called Tom.

After all, business is business.

A Good Sport

"Freddy, see you later," Arthur said as he followed my father out the paddock gate. He was riding Cricket, a mare I had purchased about three years ago. Easy to ride, she was obedient and forgiving. Arthur was game, but not very experienced. He'd be the first to say, "I'm not a natural." And he was right. I waved as they disappeared down the road.

I walked back to the barn and let the other horses out, then returned to the house. My mother was in the kitchen boiling an egg, her favorite breakfast. It was eight thirty a.m.

"Ma, when do you think they'll get back?"

"Well, you know your father." And, yes, I did know my father, whose "let's take a shortcut" always turned out to be longer than long. Today, their destination was South Woodstock, which was an easy ride if you took the dirt road. And you could get there and back in four hours. But I knew my father had other plans.

"Probably late afternoon, I imagine," I muttered. She agreed.

I opened the fridge, found an English muffin, and sliced it in two. My mother's bread was still in the toaster, so I waited.

"Okay, Freddy, it's yours," she said as she carefully removed her toast. She took her egg, toast, and coffee and disappeared into the dining room, where she and my father ate every meal. I waited for my English muffin to pop up, which it soon did, then joined her.

The day passed quickly. I schooled Martial Maid over some jumps set up in the paddock, cleaned the stalls, and did some food shopping for dinner. Davis Market was about a mile from the house, and George Davis and his wife owned and ran the place along with Junior, their only child. Junior ate too much and exercised too little, and he was creepy. Everyone tried to avoid bumping into him, but he had a knack for suddenly appearing when you paused to choose which tomato sauce to buy. Today, however, I managed to find all the ingredients on my mother's list and escape unscathed.

As we expected, my father and Arthur didn't return until two o'clock p.m. my father dismounted and opened the paddock gate. Arthur stayed mounted, and I followed them to the barn.

"Welcome back," I said, smiling broadly. Arthur didn't say a word.

"We had a wonderful ride," my father said. "He did well."

We reached the barn. I held on to Cricket as Arthur slowly slid his right leg over the saddle, draped his body over the mare, removed his left foot from the stirrup, and slid to the ground.

"Shit," he said, grimacing. "It was a long, long, long ride."

"I can imagine."

"Roger, never again," he spit out, cranking his head around to face my father. "Never again." *Oh oh,* I thought to myself. *This isn't good.* I helped Arthur untack Cricket, and we let her go. She rolled, happy to get the load off her back.

The three of us silently walked back to the house.

"Great ride," my father said to anyone who was listening. He disappeared into the living room to pour himself a large vodka.

"Arthur," he called, "something to drink?"

Arthur nodded. "Yes, whiskey."

My father filled a glass halfway with Jameson, leaving room for a few ice cubes, returned to the kitchen, and handed it to Arthur.

"Thanks," Arthur said as he sat down at the kitchen table. He took a sip, then another, and sighed.

My mother was peeling potatoes and scurrying around preparing dinner. "Roger," she said, "you have exhausted Arthur."

My father laughed, walked over to Arthur, and patted him on the back. "You'll make a cavalry man yet!" My father had spent almost two years in the cavalry at Fort Riley in Kansas riding horses, playing poker, and training for overseas duty. He had loved every minute of it and returned home an accomplished and a disciplined rider (and, may I add, skillful poker player).

"Oh no, I won't," Arthur said, staring straight at my father.

"Arthur," my mother soothingly said, "you were indeed a good sport." In my family, becoming a good sport meant you'd succeeded with honor, a huge accomplishment. But this praise flew right by Arthur, whose sense of "honor" had nothing to do with being a good sport.

"Yes, true," my father added as he disappeared into the living room to refresh his drink.

"A good sport indeed," Arthur muttered under his breath.

The years zipped by, and this "shortcut ride" to South Woodstock and back was the last time my husband Arthur and my father rode alone together.

WAS I CRAZY?

Probably!

It was another beautiful July day, sunny and cool, not too hot. I strolled around the deck, noticing that the lawn needed mowing. I'd get to it later. The red geraniums in their pots also needed attention. I'd get to that later, too.

I returned to the kitchen and poured myself another cup of coffee, added milk, and sat down on the living room couch. That was my spot. I stared at the fireplace mantel, a huge hand-hewn beam that spanned the width of the fireplace. Sitting on the top were photographs of our two sons, a box of matches, and a gold clock. Blue and white Mexican tiles surrounded the fireplace opening, defining its shape. To the right of the fireplace, the empty inset log bin stared into the living room. I opened *The Valley News*, scanned the first section, read the op-ed page and the obits. Nothing new or surprising. The funnies were next, and finally the puzzles.

At ten thirty, my son Alex and I drove to the horse barn, where my father was waiting. Why I had agreed to let Alex join us was a mystery. He was a beginner at best. And he had allergies.

I tacked up the horses. I helped Alex mount and adjusted his stirrups. Cricket was a quiet and dependable horse, but I knew enough to know that quiet and dependable horses were also horses! Again, I questioned my sanity.

I held Prompted, my father's big, brown thoroughbred, while my father, standing on the mounting block, grabbed the horse's mane, stuffed his left foot into the stirrup, and slung his right leg over the saddle. I quickly mounted Harry, a chestnut ten-year-old quarterhorse I'd bought five years ago. The three of us rode through the pasture gate and into the fields that bordered the brook.

"Alex, you look great," my father said. "Keep those heels down," he added.

Was I Crazy?

I rode in front of my father and Alex, thinking that I could take care of any mishap that might occur. Being in the front didn't guarantee anything, but at least I could control the pace. Prompted, stubborn and unpredictable, could not be trusted, nor could my father. They made a great pair.

"Frederica, should we trot?"

"No, Dad, we should not. We're sticking to a walk." Alex couldn't even post, and I thought again how crazy I was to have let him join us.

I looked behind me and smiled at twelve-year-old Alex. His brother Daniel and my husband Arthur were driving up from Cambridge, arriving around three o'clock. We planned a cookout that evening. Hamburgers and hotdogs, catsup, pickles, mustard, rolls, coleslaw, and potato salad. Ice cream for dessert.

Crows flew overhead, cawing and flapping their way across the fields. The same six or eight crows that flew above our house on the hill? Probably.

We rode along the edge of the fields. Recently hayed, they were clean and styled, like a haircut. I thought about the haircuts I had given our two sons when they were young. On the long side, their hair covered their ears and foreheads. Now, of course, they had graduated to real hair stylists. But I kept locks of their hair in an envelope tucked away in my desk drawer, along with their baby teeth.

A tractor and two empty wagons sat in the field, waiting to be picked up. The first-cut hay season had been iffy this year. Plagued with bad weather, getting in decent hay had been tough. Depending on hay for income was a tricky business.

"Frederica, here we are." We had arrived at the spot where horses and trucks and tractors crossed the brook. Shallow, but wide. I took the lead. The others followed. As I reached the other side of the brook, Alex yelled.

"Ma! Ma! Look!"

I quickly turned around. Prompted was slowly dropping into the brook, one of his great pleasures. My father kicked him hard, but Prompted paid no attention.

"Get off!" I yelled at my father. But he wasn't nimble enough, and down he went with the horse.

Cricket put her head down—she'd be next. "Oh, shit!" I jumped off, let go of Harry, and grabbed Cricket's reins.

"Alex, off!" He slid down and scrambled to the shore. And sure enough, Cricket joined Prompted in the brook before I had a chance to lead her out.

My father was struggling on his back, spurting and sputtering and yanking at his foot, which was stuck in the stirrup. Prompted tried to roll over. I grabbed

61

his reins and pushed on his side, but not too hard because had he gotten up, he would have taken off, dragging my father.

I tried to pull my father's foot out. But it had wedged itself more firmly in the stirrup. "Pull!" I yelled at my father, who tugged and tugged, but nothing worked. Prompted, now thoroughly drenched, tried to get up. Oh God. Now what? His hoofs scraped the bottom of the brook, and he thrust his legs in front of him. "Jesus!"

I tried to unbuckle the stirrup leather, but nothing budged. I reached for the girth. Could I unfasten it? No! It was stuck.

"Frederica," screamed my father, "Do something!" His face disappeared into the brook then reappeared. Frantic, I tried once again to release his foot. Prompted would be back on his feet in no time, and the only thing I could do was to hold him with my father upside down and draped against the horse's side. I knew Prompted spooked easily, and he was a strong and determined animal. Could I hold him long enough to unbuckle the girth?

Just as Prompted lurched to his feet, the stirrup leather snapped, and my father's leg fell like a rock into the stream. My father, lying on his back in the brook, pushed himself up on his elbows, coughing and spitting out water. Prompted stood quietly, probably wondering what all the fuss was about. My father rolled over onto his knees, struggled to his feet, and waded out of the brook.

Laughing, he smiled at Alex. "Great ride so far."

"Dad," I said, "we're returning to the barn."

"Why? Let's keep going. What's a little mishap?"

A little mishap?

I won this battle, and we returned to the barn, untacked the horses, rubbed them down, and let them loose into the lower pasture.

"Frederica, all's well that ends well."

"Yes, Dad."

I had been crazy after all.

ZABARSKI

My father needed a horse. His twenty-one-year-old mare was way past her prime, and it was time to replace her. He and I made some phone calls, read the horses-for-sale column in *The Chronicle of the Horse*, and visited nearby stables. No luck.

But one small ad in a local newspaper caught my eye. "Big, strong, reliable hunter for sale in Groton, Mass. Reasonably priced to a good home." My father and I hopped in the car the next day and drove to John Zabarski's modest stable in Groton.

"Hello, I'm John. How was your trip?"

"Easy," my father replied.

"Good. I'm glad." John Zabarski smiled, showing a gap between his upper front teeth. Slightly bow-legged, compact, wiry, and probably in his late 60s, he was a man of few words. He wore jeans, half chaps, and brown jodhpur boots. His bright yellow shirt, open at his neck, fit him snugly, and a robin's-egg blue scarf was loosely tied around his neck. He reminded me of our bantam rooster.

"By the way, do you know Stacey and Sybil Benson?"

"Of course I do," John said. "They're close friends of mine and stalwart members of the Groton Hunt."

"They are indeed," said my father. "Frederica and I often hunt at Groton, and the Bensons visit us at least once a year in Vermont for long riding weekends. They're great sports." And great sports they needed to be to follow my father cross-country. "Let's take a shortcut" meant leaving the dirt roads and well-worn bridle paths behind and heading into the country. My father luckily had an uncanny sense of direction, but getting from point A to point

B was always an adventure. Barbed wire never stopped him. He'd just hang his jacket over the wire. "We'll just pop over."

"Yes, great sports," John said. "I no longer hunt because of my arthritic back. Now I only hack short distances, hence my selling Big Boy, the horse you're looking at."

John led through to his immaculately kept barn—the middle aisle swept clean, halters and shanks neatly hung beside each of the four stalls, and blankets draped over metal bars. Three horses peered out of their stalls as we strolled down the aisle.

"Here he is," John said. Big Boy whinnied as we approached, his ears pricked forward. He was enormous, over 17 hands high, with a beautiful roan-and-chestnut coat. I rubbed his nose and looked into his large kind eyes. I liked this horse.

John cross-tied him and tacked him up, then did the same for a smaller bay mare for himself. My father trusted my judgment, so he asked me to ride the horse. I agreed.

John and I mounted, and I followed him out of the pasture down a dirt road and into the woods. Before long we were galloping along at a fairly good clip. Big Boy was energetic and eager and alert. And he was comfortable, something that my father would like.

After a half hour or so, we returned to the barn. John dismounted, as did I. "What do you think?" My father looked at me, eyebrows raised and head tilted. "He's great," I replied. I filled him in, explaining where we'd been and how the horse had handled himself—and, above all, how comfortable his gaits were.

"He's yours," John said, "for one hundred dollars." My father and I looked at each other and smiled. "A deal," my father said.

We unsaddled the horses and put a blanket on Big Boy. My father made out a check for one hundred dollars and handed it to John, who folded it in half and stuffed it in his back pocket. He wrote out a receipt, which he and my father signed. We loaded Big Boy into the trailer and headed home.

"Hmm," my father said. "Big Boy? Can we come up with another name?"

"Absolutely." I said. "How about Zabarski?"

"Zabarski it is!" And the name stuck.

We were pleased with Zabarski, whose temperament and manners were exemplary; he was a real gentleman in and around the barn, and at over 17 hands, his presence was impressive. The other four horses got along with him, and the barn was a happy place for the horses, the barn cats, and the three bantam chickens. A donkey soon joined the crowd, plus an almost blind pony given to my father by a local farmer.

Everyone loved Zabarski, and my father enjoyed this horse more than all the others he had owned. Even though the horse was enormous, his size never interfered with his sure footedness; he rarely stumbled. My father hunted him safely, as well as rode him cross-country alone or with me—always with confidence. Zabarski easily jumped stone walls, forded streams, and never spooked.

When Zabarski turned seventeen, we noticed he was off in front. The vet came and told us, to our dismay, that he had laminitis, which we tried to control for a while, but unfortunately it became chronic and untreatable. "You'll have to put him down," our vet said. "He's in pain, and I can't do anything more for him."

Zabarski soon joined the other horses in our lower pasture's horse graveyard. It was a sad day for us. When we walked into the barn after burying him, we could tell that the horses, the cats, the bantam chickens, the donkey, and the pony felt his absence, too.

I know Zabarski sits with honor in horse heaven, and why wouldn't he?

PITCHFORK

I sipped my coffee and watched the mist creep up the mountain like the slow, gentle lifting of a wedding veil. The mountain was beautiful this time of year in Vermont, when the October leaves flash their red and yellow colors. A cool breeze touched my face. It felt good.

Down in the lower meadow, the wild turkeys pecked their way across the field. There must have been about twenty of them. I remember last spring when they were babies, following their mothers like obedient soldiers.

Nobody was up; the house was still. The coffee mug warmed my hands. I lifted it to my lips, carefully sipping the coffee and feeling its heat. My thoughts drifted here and there, and I turned inward, listening to my breath. Closing my eyes, I felt very much at peace with the world.

Until the phone rang. I entered the house through the sliding door and picked up the phone.

"Frederica, good morning."

"Good morning."

"What a beautiful day," he said.

"Yes," I replied as I sat down. I lay my right hand, fingers spread, on the dining room table.

"A perfect day for a ride."

"Uh, well, I don't know, Dad. I'll have to check with the others; I'm not sure exactly what the plans are, what's going on today."

"Frederica, it's such a lovely day—it would be a pity to waste it."

"I know, but I need to check first. It may be okay, but it will have to be a short ride."

"Well, we'll see," my father said.

I shifted in my chair.

"Meet me at the barn at ten o'clock, and we'll decide then."

"Alright." I picked up my coffee cup and returned to the deck. The mist had lifted, and the mountain was in full view. I studied it, following the skyline down its right side past the towers. The ski trails hung from the first ridge, peeping out here and there as they descended the face. I had skied this mountain since I was a little girl, pigtails popping out from under my hat. My father had taught me to ski. I smiled. The ambivalence caught me off guard.

At ten o'clock, I drove the grey pickup down the hill and parked at the entrance to the barn. My father was in the tack room. He wore his worn tweed jacket with patched leather elbows, a yellow scarf tied around his neck, and cavalry breeches, which had been taken out at the back seams at least four inches. The repair fit the man and didn't seem odd at all.

"Good morning, Frederica."

"Good morning."

"What a day!"

"Yes, it is," I replied.

"We won't be out for more than an hour or so. We'll just ride to Sheddsville and back." My father looked at me, and I nodded.

He sat down on the old folding chair near the bureau. He removed the wooden boot trees from his Cavalry boots and placed them on the floor.

He looked up. "Frederica, the horses are in. Why don't you tack them up while I get my boots on."

I unbolted the stall door of Prompted, the big thoroughbred given to my father by friends in Virginia. He was gorgeous, almost 17 hands high, towering above the other horses. Prompted pricked up his ears as I entered the stall, and I whispered to him as he rubbed up against me. I attached the halter shank, led him out of the stall, and cross-tied him. His skin rippled as I brushed him. He was sensitive. I picked up each of his feet and cleaned them out with a hoof pick. I had to lean into him before he would pick up his hind feet; he had a stubborn streak. I saddled him up, careful not to tighten the girth too quickly or too tightly. Prompted hated that.

I did the same for Cricket, a half-bred I had bought years ago. She was an honest horse, and I liked her for that. I looped the reins around the stirrup leathers of each saddle and returned the horses to their stalls.

"All set," I said as I returned to the tack room.

"I'll be out in a minute," my father replied. He was in the bathroom, where I knew he was smoothing his eyebrows and checking his fly. In the tiny bathroom were also cans of nails, screws, bolts and washers, which sat on a narrow shelf, and a hammer, screwdriver and pliers that hung between nails on the bathroom wall. Above the toilet a cracked mirror was suspended from a nail.

I walked back to the horses and adjusted the throat latches and girths. Prompted nipped at me as I tightened his girth one more hole. I left the two horses in their stalls and walked to the wide-open door. The sun peeked into the barn and settled on my black boots. I walked a few steps further and listened to the water splash against the rocks bordering the small stream that meandered through the pasture.

"Frederica, I can't seem to get my spurs on," my father yelled from the tack room.

"Coming." I walked back into the tack room and saw him struggling with his left spur.

"I'll do that." I leaned over and pulled the strap through the small buckle, fastening it at the worn place, and did the same thing with his right spur.

"I must be getting old," my father said, standing up. "I'll be out in a minute," he added as he returned to the bathroom. I hoped he'd be able to button up his fly. His cavalry breeches had many tiny buttons.

I led Prompted out of his stall to the mounting block, which stood unceremoniously between the manure pile and the barn. My father appeared, holding his crop in his right hand. He walked to the mounting block and climbed the two steps.

"Do you have him?"

"Yes, I do."

I held the reins and pulled down hard on the right stirrup leather, waiting for the weight of my father as he stepped into the left stirrup. Prompted edged away from the mounting block. "Damn," my father said.

I pushed Prompted's hind quarters back. "Okay, go ahead," I said. Prompted heaved as my father pulled himself over the horse's back and landed heavily into the saddle.

"Can you check my girth, Frederica?"

I pushed my father's leg forward, lifted the saddle skirt, and pulled hard on the billet straps, moving the buckles up another couple of holes. My father collected the reins and urged Prompted away from the mounting block. I returned to the barn, led Cricket out, mounted quickly, and easily tightened her girth. We left the barn at 10:45.

Cricket and Prompted walked through the pasture gate and crossed Route

44 onto the dirt road that led to Sheddsville. I returned my gaze to the mountain and the big tower on the top, the tower I had climbed many times.

My father's thoroughbred followed my mare up the long hill. At the top, we turned left through the gap in the wall, a shortcut to Sam Brown's huge field, where a few stray rotting hay bales remained. His equipment was still there.

"Shall we move along?"

Urging his big horse into a canter and then a gallop, my father headed for the corner of the field. I watched the back of his torn tweed jacket flap up and down, like a wounded bird trying to get off the ground.

I soon caught up with him, and we galloped side by side. The wind felt cold but fresh. I should have worn my old green wool sweater instead of the cotton one. At the top of the field, we slowed down to a trot and then a walk and entered the woods. We followed a well-trodden trail fondly called "The White Birches" because these beautiful trees grew in clumps on either side of the trail. Their copper-colored leaves chattered against the wind. Soon they'd be lying on the ground, waiting for snow.

I had cross-country skied here many times, lunch in my knapsack. I always sat on a fallen tree that rarely got buried by snow, enjoying my carefully wrapped Cheddar sandwich, an apple or pear, and a few pieces of chocolate. The menu rarely changed, and the only sounds I ever heard were my own.

"Frederica, I need to take a leak."

I was never completely prepared for this announcement even though it happened every time we rode together, especially in these later years. I dismounted and led Prompted to a slight bank and held tightly to the reins. My father dragged his right leg over the saddle, pulled his left food out of the iron, and slid down the side of the horse. I watched his legs buckle slightly as they hit the ground.

"God, I'm getting old," he said as he walked stiffly to the edge of the path.

The thin spray of yellow urine landed on leaves that fluttered under the pressure. In a minute or so, my father's legs spread slightly. "Shit," he said. I didn't say a word. I knew he was struggling with the buttons on his fly.

"That's better," he finally said. He walked back to Prompted, checked his girth and leathers. My father handed me his reins and clambered up the bank. I pushed Prompted as close to the bank as I could.

"Are you ready?" I asked him.

"Do you have him?"

He slipped his left foot into the stirrup and grabbed the mane.

"You have him?"

"Yes," I replied, pulling on the right leather and leaning against the horse.

My father swung his leg over the saddle. Prompted sank under my father's weight, shifting his own weight to steady himself.

"Double check my girth, Frederica."

I checked both girths and then mounted Cricket. The path turned right into a large, open meadow. When we reached the top, we stopped to admire the breathtaking 360-degree view. Both horses stood quietly, happy for the rest.

"Beautiful," said my father.

I nodded and wriggled my toes in my boots, remembering that my father had these made for me in Kansas. My very first pair were jodhpur boots, which he had bought me when he returned from the war in 1946. I was eight years old.

"You'll need these, Frederica, because you're getting a pony."

Honey, a black-and-white friendly but willful Shetland pony, arrived soon after. I loved riding her around and around the enclosed paddock until she decided enough was enough. Honey was always in charge. When I turned ten, I graduated to Big Mare, my father's 16.2-hand horse. I had to reach way up to saddle her, but she always stood quietly while I fumbled around. I often rode Big Mare to my best friend's farm on weekends, weather permitting. Together, Sandy on Sport and I on Big Mare, would head to the nearby brook, tie the horses up, and swim. After returning to her farm, we'd spend hours cantering up and down the dirt road in front of her house, dust flying. On Sundays, after filling up with homemade blueberry pancakes drowned in maple syrup, I'd ride the five miles home. What happy days those were!

"Shall we go?" Startled, I turned my head and looked at my father. He had already started down the other side of the meadow.

"Yes," I replied. We soon entered a forgotten pasture now filled with juniper bushes. Our two horses wove their way down to the dirt road below. Turning right, my father urged his horse into a trot. Soon we reached Sheddsville, a small cluster of houses established around 1768 by members of the Shedd family. Even though more houses had been added over the years, Sheddsville maintained that community kinship typical of many other small Vermont hamlets.

As I was turning left to head for home, my father interrupted my thoughts.

"Wait a minute, I want to take a small detour."

"What? Detour? Where?"

"Not far; I'd like to look for that old logging road that connects the Smith's field to the McClary's."

"Dad, I need to get home."

"This won't take long," my father replied.

I followed him up the dirt road, and, in a few hundred feet, he turned right into the Smith's field. I looked at my watch; we'd already been gone for well over an hour. We rode around the field, looking for the entrance to the logging road but found nothing.

"Then let's head for home," I said.

"Alright," my father said.

We left the field and headed down the dirt road. We finally reached the last field before finally arriving home. This field belonged to neighbors, dairy farmers. I looked at my watch again, shifted my position, and urged Cricket forward.

At last, we walked through the pasture gate and toward the mounting block. I slipped off my horse and led her into her stall. I returned to the mounting block and took hold of the reins.

"Careful," my father said. "Push him over."

I leaned against Prompted as my father slipped his right foot out of the stirrup. With a giant effort, he pulled his leg over the saddle, and it landed safely on the block. I helped him release his left foot from the stirrup and then to the ground. I led Prompted into the aisle, replaced the bridle with a halter, and cross-tied him. After loosening the girth, I removed the saddle and took it and the bridle into the tack room to be cleaned. I sponged him off, checked his legs, and let him go. I did the same for Cricket. Both horses rolled in the barnyard. That must have felt good, I thought.

"Frederica, are the horses out?"

"Yes."

I returned to the tack room. My father was sitting on the chair, fumbling with his spurs.

"Frederica, can you help me?" I leaned over and pulled one strap, releasing the buckle on one spur, and did the same for the other. I hung both spurs on their hook.

"Now, my boots," my father said. Turning my back to him, I grabbed one boot between my legs and pulled. My father grunted, leaning back, resisting my pull. His foot slipped out of the boot, always more slowly than I wanted. The second boot was more difficult. Its hard leather toe jammed into my crotch as I thrust all my weight forward.

"Pull, Frederica." And I did, with all my might. With a sudden jerk, the boot released my father's foot. I stood up and placed both boots in front of my father, who carefully inserted the wooden boot trees. Standing up, he placed the boots next to the yellow bureau, where they would wait patiently for the next ride. He slipped on his rubber boots, stood up, and walked to the sink with a sponge. After cleaning off the bits, my father started on the bridles. I knew he would unbuckle each strap, prolonging a job I could do in minutes.

"Great ride, Frederica. Next time, we'll take the trailer and head up to the Reeves."

"Sounds nice."

My father disappeared into the bathroom, and I heard the soft tinkle of pee and hoped he hadn't missed the toilet. I finished cleaning the saddles, returned them to their racks, hung up the girths, and waited.

"I guess we're all done," I said as my father emerged from the bathroom. "Great ride. Horses out?"

At one thirty, we climbed the steep stairs to the top of the barn. I followed my father, who clung to the rail as he slowly put one foot in front of the other. At the top, he turned right and headed for the door.

As I approached the opening, I noticed the steel pitchfork leaning against the wall, tongs up. I touched its cold tynes and shivered.

THE PHONE CALL

"Hello?"

"Frederica, it's me, Betsy."

I rarely answered phone calls when I was teaching, but Betsy was one of three caregivers who looked after my parents. And Betsy didn't usually call with good news.

"It's your father." She paused. "He had an accident." Another pause. "And didn't make it."

I took a deep breath. "You mean he's dead?"

Betsy had heard a crash and found my father at the bottom of the stairs. She phoned Ralph, a neighbor, who rushed over then called an ambulance.

I looked into the classroom, the students hard at work. The clock hanging on my office wall said three forty-five. In fifteen minutes, class would be over.

"Betsy, I'll call Connie, and we'll drive right up. How's Ma?" My mother had suffered a series of strokes that profoundly affected her speech and comprehension. She had no words and understood only a little of what was said.

"She's upset," Betsy said. "I'll stay with her until you arrive. She's sitting in your father's chair and won't move. She knows."

"Okay." I told her we'd be up in about three hours. I called my sister Connie and then my brother Nick, who was bicycling across the country. He'd hop on a plane.

It was early October. My husband and I always spend July and August in Vermont; we lived five miles from my parents' house, which was in Reading. My father had been sober all summer. About three times a week, I enjoyed a cup of tea and a game of cribbage with my father, an enthusiastic and smart player. He could beat you with lousy hands.

Sometimes, I'd drive him to our house and show him the new horse I had bought a few months ago. My father, a horseman through and through, had approved of my purchase. We often sat in the tack room and chatted about the old days when horses filled his barn and our lives. Now 85 years old, he and my mother had recently moved to a smaller house in the village. All his horses were gone, either sold or given away. But we had our memories, and I had my horse.

I also took my mother on drives, stopping for a vanilla ice cream cone, her favorite. The ice cream always drizzled down her chin, but we laughed as I cleaned her up. She beamed and nodded her head and made noises that told me everything was fine. The summer had been a happy few months.

In late August, when I returned to Cambridge and my job, things began to fall apart. "Frederica," phoned Betsy, "your father is drinking again. I can deal with it, just wanted you to know the situation." The weeks went by, the phone calls increased, and things got worse.

Connie and I arrived at seven thirty. Betsy greeted us at the kitchen door. We noticed glasses drying on the rack and two empty wine bottles. "He finished both," said Emma, another caregiver.

Ralph stood by the living room door. "He was lying here," he said, pointing to the rug at the bottom of the stairs. "I don't think he suffered," he added.

My mother was sitting in my father's chair, a faded yellow velvet wingback, next to the fire. Her eyes fell on us, and she wept and flailed her arms. Connie pulled a chair next to her and held her hands. I hugged her and rubbed her back. "Ma," I said, "it's going to be alright." She nodded, tears flowing down her cheeks. "I know," I said. "We're staying. We'll take care of everything." I looked down. On her feet were my father's ratty old sheepskin L.L. Bean slippers, which he'd kept next to the chair.

We thanked Ralph, who had to leave. "I was happy to do what I could," he said. "Let me know if there is anything else." He put on his coat and walked out the door.

Emma and Betsy left, as well, also offering help. "Stew on the stove," Emma said.

Connie and I returned to the living room. Ma pointed to the stairs and uttered sounds that just poured out. "Ma," I said, "we're here." I wrapped my arms around her, her bony shoulders hunching forward into my arms. I held her tight. "Ma, it's okay."

As my mother slowly wiped away her tears with one hand, Connie gently finished the job with my father's frayed white handkerchief, clutched in Ma's other hand. I called the funeral home and said we'd come in the morning.

It was dark and cold outside. I covered my mother's knees with a wool blanket, tucking it in. The furnace had gone out, so we added more logs to the fire, giving us some warmth, but not much. It was a hard night.

At the funeral home, Mr. Bent greeted us warmly. I had gone to grammar school with his son, Larry, so we exchanged a few nostalgic memories. In the basement, my father was lying on a gurney. Jeff, Connie's husband, and Nick had arrived, and they stood in the doorway, waiting for their turn to say goodbye.

I put my hand on my father's chest. A few buttons were missing from his faded, blue Brooks Brothers shirt, so I closed the openings, giving him a neater look. Caked blood covered his broken nose. He had a black eye, the purple shade drifting onto his left cheek. Two ragged cuts on his forehead would probably have required stitches. His body was as still as a fallen tree, but I still searched his face for something, not sure what. Maybe a tiny smile? Or a raised eyebrow? Nothing. His hands rested by his side, like dead branches. His nails needed to be cut; Betsy would have taken care of that.

"Dad," I said out loud, "alcoholism is a terrible thing; you did the best you could."

I stared at the far wall, thinking about all the other people who had lain on this same gurney. My father was just another body.

I looked at my father and smiled. "Bye, Dad, hang in there. You're okay now." And I left the room.

About the Author

Frederica Steinberg, now retired, taught English at the Cambridge School of Weston and writing at Lesley University and MIT. She also ran tutoring and weaving businesses.

In 2019, Steinberg and her husband Arthur published *Soul of Venice*, a novel set in Venice, Italy. In 2023, she published a book of poems, *A Good Life*, about Arthur's illness and death.

Steinberg competed in equestrian events when she was younger, and she continued to ride in the Vermont countryside until a few years ago when she sold her last horse.

Steinberg has two sons, Alex and Daniel, and four grandchildren, Jake, Maya, Julia, and Jack.